The Ultimate Sight Reading Music Manual

A Proven System to Read Music Effortlessly & Bring Notation to Life – Gain Accuracy & Artistry at Adequate Tempos + Conquer Every Hidden Sight-Reading Obstacle

Luciano Marazzo

The Online Music Guild via Ascoltando Inc

ISBNs
eBook: 978-631-00-8017-8
Paperback: 978-631-00-7869-4
Hardcover: 978-631-00-8211-0
Audiobook: 978-631-00-8210-3

CONTENTS

A Note from the Author

Luciano Marazzo

If you've ever struggled with sight-reading, you're not alone. It's frustrating to see the notes in front of you but feel like they're slipping through your fingers. You know you're capable of more, yet something just isn't clicking. Here's what most musicians don't hear enough: it's not because you lack talent.

This book was originally written for classical musicians—players who face the relentless demands of orchestral rehearsals, auditions, and intricate scores. But as it grew, something became clear: sight-reading isn't just a classical music skill—it's a musician's skill. Whether you play jazz, rock, pop, or any other genre, the core challenges of sight-reading remain the same. If it hasn't worked for you yet, it's not because you're bad at it. It's because somewhere along the way, you were missing a piece of the puzzle.

This book is about uncovering those missing pieces—not just for sight-reading, but for your musicianship as a whole. As I wrote, I realized something unexpected: these skills don't just make you a better musician. They sharpen your reflexes, your confidence, and your ability to think ahead. They improve your ability to handle mistakes, adapt, and thrive in high-pressure situations—on stage and in life.

Somewhere along the way, this book came to life on its own. What started as a structured guide for sight-reading evolved into something deeper—a resource for musicians who want to break past their limitations, no matter their genre or background. What if, just a few chapters from now, sight-reading started to feel different? More natural? More instinctive? What if you could sit down with a new piece of music and, instead of dreading it, welcome the challenge? Read this book not just with mere curiosity, but with the confidence that you are capable of far much more than you can imagine.

This book is dedicated...

To my children: the source of my greatest strength, inspiration, and joy. This work is for you to be inspired to always keep learning.

To my parents, who nurtured my passion for music. This work is thanks to the amazing education and upbringing you have given me.

To the musicians collaborating in this project: thank you for putting my ideas under extreme fire, pressure, and scrutiny. You have helped me make diamonds.

To my friends, teachers, and colleagues who have always supported me. This work is a tribute to your kindness and love.

To all the wise individuals who believe in the transformative power of music. May this work inspire you to continue working hard seeking your ultimate potential.

FOREWORD

BY GUSTAVO BEAKLINI

IN AUGUST 2009, I had the unexpected privilege of meeting Luciano Marazzo. We found ourselves seated side by side at the Orientation for International Students in one of the largest halls at the University of Arizona. The room was filled with students from across the globe, and the atmosphere was buzzing with anticipation and uncertainty. Amid the sea of faces, it seemed improbable that two musicians would cross paths. Luciano was the first to break the ice, greeting me with a warm smile. What began as a casual introduction quickly grew into a meaningful connection. Over the following weeks, we encountered one another at various orientations for teaching assistants and the School of Music. Through those interactions, we became colleagues and eventually close friends.

At 23, I had just won two major solo competitions in Brazil and was starting my role as a Harp Teaching Assistant in one of the largest harp departments in the United States. After my studies in Arizona, I returned to Brazil to establish harp programs at two conservatories while maintaining an active career as a performer and educator. Luciano's path was equally remarkable. He founded a thriving online community of musicians, performed operas and guitar recitals internationally, delivered a TEDx talk, and now—as an author—shares his wisdom through this book.

The Ultimate Sight-Reading Music Book showcases Luciano's dedication to helping musicians excel. Sight-reading, as he passionately asserts, is an invaluable skill that separates great musicians from exceptional ones. The ability to play music directly from the page is not just a technical proficiency but a professional necessity. It opens doors to last-minute gigs, enhances collaboration, and is a hallmark of adaptability in the fast-paced world of performance.

In this book, Luciano unpacks the complexity of sight-reading with clarity and precision. Drawing from years of experience and research, he breaks down the skill into manageable components, offering strategies to build fluency and confidence. Whether you are a beginner or a seasoned performer, the tools provided here will guide you toward mastering this essential aspect of musicianship.

One of the book's most powerful lessons is learning to let go of mistakes—a principle that extends beyond music. Luciano's insight reminds us that perfection is not the goal; rather, it is the ability to move forward with passion and authenticity that defines true artistry. His approach balances technical rigor with the human element of music, encouraging readers to embrace both discipline and expression.

I am honored to introduce this book, which I believe will inspire and equip countless musicians. Luciano's dedication, creativity, and relentless pursuit of excellence shine through every page. I invite you to immerse yourself in this journey and discover how sight-reading can transform your musical life.

Gustavo Beaklini

OVERTURE

READ THIS FIRST

"Imagine sitting down in front of a brand-new piece of music. Within seconds, your eyes scan patterns, your brain interprets them, your hands move instinctively, and your ears fine-tune your performance. Sight-reading is not just about seeing notes—it's a synchronized process of perception, decision-making, and execution. And like any skill, it can be mastered."

Introduction

IF YOU'RE HOLDING THIS book in your hands, chances are you already know that your sight-reading skills could use some improvement. Maybe you've spent countless hours practicing.

Yet, the moment you're faced with an unfamiliar piece of music, everything seems to fall apart. Perhaps you've convinced yourself that sight-reading is some mystical ability that only a chosen few are born with. If that sounds familiar, let me assure you—you're not alone.

Or maybe you're just starting your musical journey and haven't yet faced the challenge of sight-reading. Right now, the dots and lines on the page may still feel new and exciting, and you're eager to get everything right. That excitement is a great place to start, but having a plan to develop solid sight-reading habits from the beginning will save you from years of frustration.

And then, there are those reading this book not for themselves, but because they see someone struggling—perhaps a student, a friend, a child, or a colleague. Watching a musician wrestle with sight-reading can be frustrating, especially when you know they have the talent to play beautifully. Whether you're a teacher looking for better ways to help your students, a parent who wants to support a child's music education, or simply someone who wants to support a musician they care about, this book will serve as a valuable resource.

Sight-reading isn't just playing one note at a time—it's scanning patterns, predicting structure, and making split-second decisions. Processing, interpreting, and executing are challenging tasks: a complex interplay of visual recognition, mental processing, muscle coordination, and auditory feedback. Some musicians develop these skills quickly, but for most, the key isn't just more practice—it's diagnosing and fine-tuning the hidden factors that hinder sight-reading, like a clock-maker adjusting gears to ensure perfect precision.If you've struggled with it, that doesn't mean you're not talented or that something is wrong—it simply means you haven't yet approached it in a way that truly works for you. That's exactly what this book will help you change.

This book is designed to help you examine all the variables in the sight-reading process. It examines sight-reading from every angle, uncovering the hidden obstacles that might hinder your ability to read music with fluidity. Some concepts might seem simple, but the real breakthroughs happen when you start paying attention to what has been overlooked. By the end of this journey, you will have a clear framework for improving sight-reading. Not through guesswork, but through proven and effective strategies.

Why do we need this skill?

Now that we've identified the challenges of sight-reading, let's explore why mastering it is transformative. Sight-reading grants musicians spontaneity and professionalism, allowing them to approach new pieces with confidence. Whether stepping in last-minute, sight-reading at rehearsal, or tackling unfamiliar repertoire without extensive preparation, this skill provides the freedom to adapt and succeed. Stronger sight-reading means more gigs, smoother collaborations, and greater confidence—making it one of the most valuable tools a musician can develop.

For professionals, it's the difference between being in demand or missing opportunities. For students, it determines whether they excel in lessons or constantly feel behind. Educators who truly understand sight-reading can teach students to read fluently—not just play from memory. Yet many musicians, beginners and pros alike, claim, *"I just don't have the knack for it"* or rely on memorization instead. But sight-reading isn't a rare talent—it's an essential skill that any well-rounded musician can develop.

So why does it feel so difficult? Because sight-reading isn't just about repetition—it's about real-time decision-making. Traditional practice methods focus on familiarity, not adaptability. If you've practiced for hours yet still struggle to sight-read, the issue isn't talent—it's the approach. Mastering sight-reading requires a shift in strategy, focusing on rapid pattern recognition, real-time processing, and structured techniques designed for fluency.

Extended Complimentary Resources

This book is designed for rapid transformation—not a bloated academic text filled with fluff. In just a few hours, you'll pinpoint exactly what's been holding you back in sight-reading and learn how to fix it permanently. But knowledge alone isn't enough—you need a clear, structured path to mastery.

That's where our Extended Complimentary Resources come in. This QR code unlocks a massive library of progressive sight-reading materials—not generic drills, but instrument-specific training for pianists, violinists, guitarists, flutists, harpists, and more. You'll also find warm-ups, challenge modules, and printable tracking tools designed to accelerate real-world fluency across all experience levels.

While we recommend reading the book first, you can scan the QR code anytime to request access and be ready to work as soon as you finish reading the book.

What's Inside?

Progressive Training Plans → One exercise per day, structured from absolute beginner to master level, eliminating guesswork.

Personalized Practice Journal → Plan, track, and refine your sessions with built-in self-assessment prompts.

The Extended Finale Self-Assessment → A deeper dive into your strengths, weaknesses, and breakthroughs.

Ongoing, Exclusive Content Updates → New exercises & refinements added regularly, so your progress never stops.

The three sections of the book

This book is structured into three sections, each designed to build a complete and strategic approach to sight-reading mastery.

Section One: The Foundations

The first section lays the groundwork, connecting technical mastery, music theory, and music history to real-time execution. These elements shape how we recognize patterns, interpret phrasing, and translate notation into sound. Without them, sight-reading feels like guessing; with them, it becomes structured and intuitive. This section ensures that every aspect of your musicianship supports and strengthens your ability to read, understand, and perform music at first sight.

Section Two: Execution Strategies

The second section focuses on practical strategies for execution, providing a structured approach to navigating a score efficiently. You'll learn to scan scores effectively, identify key elements, and set the right tempo before playing. Developing these habits leads to greater accuracy, fluency, and control, transforming sight-reading from a guessing game into a deliberate, strategic process. With consistent application, these techniques become second nature, allowing you to approach any piece with confidence and precision.

Section Three: The Mindset for Mastery

The final section explores the mental and personal aspects of musicianship, focusing on confidence, adaptability, and resilience. Sight-reading isn't just about technical skill—it requires the right mindset. This section will help you stay composed under pressure, embrace challenges, and refine your musical intuition. By strengthening your focus, emotional balance, and learning approach, you'll gain the tools to overcome obstacles, accelerate progress, and deepen your connection to music.

While this book is centered on sight-reading, its principles extend to all areas of musicianship. The strategies you learn will refine your technical control, musical phrasing, and performance confidence. Whether you're reading from the page, playing from memory, or rehearsing with an ensemble, these concepts will enhance your ability to perform with versatility, expression, and adaptability.

The benefits of sight-reading

Many musicians struggle with self-doubt, frustration, and fear of mistakes, but sight-reading—like all performance skills—is as much about mindset as it is about ability. Overcoming hesitation, staying focused, and developing resilience are essential to mastering it. Fluent sight-reading sets musicians apart, making them adaptable, reliable, and invaluable in any setting. Whether stepping in for a sick performer or tackling an unfamiliar score in rehearsal, strong sight-reading skills turn uncertainty into opportunity, ensuring you're always prepared for any musical challenge.

Sight-reading unlocks endless musical possibilities, allowing you to explore new repertoire, composers, and styles without extensive preparation. It builds resilience, teaching you to adapt, recover from mistakes, and push forward with confidence. But beyond its practical benefits, sight-reading cultivates humility, patience, and discipline, reinforcing that music is both an art and a lifelong pursuit. The journey of improving this skill is just as valuable as the skill itself, sharpening focus, adaptability, and self-reflection—qualities that elevate every aspect of your musicianship.

Challenges Ahead

> *"At the heart of sight-reading lies a battle between confidence and hesitation. The mind reacts to unfamiliar music by either adapting or freezing. The difference isn't talent—it's mindset."*

Mastering sight-reading comes with challenges: impatience and self-doubt being the most common. Impatience arises when progress feels slow, but like any skill, sight-reading requires consistency and trust in the process. Every small improvement lays the foundation for lasting growth. Self-doubt fuels hesitation, making new challenges feel overwhelming. This book will help you break through those two and many other obstacles, providing strategies to build confidence, stay focused, and develop a mindset that fosters steady progress and resilience.

The following nine chapters will do more than just teach you to play notes; they will strengthen your rhythm, timing, interpretation, and critical thinking in real time. They refine your ability to make split-second decisions and challenge you to look deep within yourself—transforming every negative variable into an asset that works in your favor. By balancing technical precision with emotional expression, sight-reading deepens your connection to music, making you a more adaptable, expressive, and confident musician.

A Transformative Journey

By the end of this book, you'll see sight-reading as both a process and an art form. You will know the path to read music with clarity and confidence. This journey isn't about perfection—it's about becoming the best musician you can be. Sight-reading will serve you throughout your career, unlocking new opportunities and experiences.

We are on a path to re-train your complete approach and relationship to music in general. Are you ready to put in the work to make that transformation happen? With the right approach, progress will come faster than you expect. This book will be your guide, providing insights, techniques, and encouragement to help you succeed.

As you turn the page, remember: Every musician starts somewhere. But today, you're not just reading a book—you're building your future as a musician. Every skill you develop here is a key, unlocking doors to opportunities you never even imagined.

SECTION ONE

The Fundamental Skills

Introduction

Just like when baking a cake, mastering sight-reading starts with the best ingredients—clear, high-quality, and precisely measured. Before we can bake, we must develop each ingredient to its fullest potential. This section ensures that every element is identified, refined, and ready to be combined into a seamless skill. That's why Chapters 1, 2, and 3 go together: Chapter 1 explores the process, Chapter 2 builds the knowledge behind it, and Chapter 3 focuses on the mastering your instrument so it can bring everything together.

This section is the first step to embed sight-reading into your subconscious, transforming it from a conscious effort into an automatic skill. It's mastery requires a strategic and deliberate approach that we outline clearly throughout the entire book. Your success relies on the foundation you build. A key part of this foundation is understanding how the brain acquires and retains information—a process rooted in neuro-plasticity. Experts in learning science identify four distinct stages of competence, each marking a crucial step in skill development.

Unconscious Incompetence
Conscious Incompetence
Conscious Competence
Unconscious Competence

This book will guide you toward unconscious competence in sight-reading, transforming it into an effortless skill. By sharpening awareness, deepening understanding, and refining technique, you'll develop the ability to interpret and execute music instinctively. Sight-reading will become second nature, seamlessly integrated into your musical subconscious for fluid, confident performance.

The Importance of Awareness

Stepping back to see the bigger picture is key to mastering sight-reading. Like a puzzle, we start by building the frame before filling in the details. Instead of getting caught in the frustration of slow progress, awareness helps you form a clear action plan to remove friction from the sight-reading process. Many musicians feel stuck and turn to memorization to compensate. While memorization is essential for music in general, it does not make someone a strong sight-reader. Without refining sight-reading, opportunities in a competitive field become limited.

Awareness is the first step to mastery—it allows you to pinpoint the obstacles that gum up the engine of sight-reading. By stepping back, you can identify inefficiencies, eliminate friction, and focus on what truly drives progress—not just playing accurately, but reading fluently. Awareness enables continuous growth, transforming sight-reading into an effortless process. By actively refining this skill, you bridge the gap between your current abilities and mastery, making sight-reading a seamless and indispensable part of your musicianship.

Breaking the Sight-Reading Barrier

You have completed countless sight-reading exercises, yet the results have led you here. Without addressing what is missing, repetition alone will not make sight-reading easier. When writing this book, we deliberately chose to exclude drills from its core. Instead, our focus is to guide you in identifying and correcting the fundamental gaps that hinder progress. Many musicians default to memorization—not by choice, but due to unseen weaknesses in their sight-reading foundation.

This section dissects the fundamental building blocks of sight-reading, leaving you with no choice but to evaluate yourself. Yet awareness alone is not enough—progress comes from action. Sight-reading does not improve by merely identifying obstacles but by systematically addressing them. Every limitation you uncover is an opportunity for growth. Recognize the problem, commit to resolving it, and turn uncertainty into confidence.

Strengthening Your Musical Core

Strengthening your foundation means refining the essential ingredients of sight-reading. Music theory, history, and instrumental mastery are not separate concepts—they are the core elements that make fluent reading possible. Without them, sight-reading remains unstable, forcing you to rely on instinct instead of understanding, reaction instead of control.

This stage is about deepening your command of these elements so they work together, rather than in isolation. Music theory sharpens recognition, history shapes interpretation, and instrumental mastery ensures precision. The goal is not just to improve but to remove friction, allowing sight-reading to become fluid, confident, and adaptable in any musical setting. The stronger your foundation, the more effortlessly you will navigate new music, transforming sight-reading from a challenge into an instinct.

Unlocking Fluency in Sight-Reading

A solid foundation is essential, but it is not enough. The first three chapters develop the core ingredients of sight-reading—building awareness, identifying gaps, and refining fundamental skills. But ingredients alone do not create mastery. Without the right methodology, habits, and mindset, these elements remain disconnected, keeping sight-reading from becoming a truly effortless skill.

Unconscious competence is the ultimate goal—where reading music becomes is driven into a carefully developed yet natural instinct, in other words, it becomes second nature. Section One establishes the groundwork for this transformation, ensuring that every essential element is developed with clarity and precision. Without this foundation, progress remains inconsistent, and mastery stays out of reach. As you move forward, Sections Two and Three will refine your approach, discipline, and adaptability, shaping sight-reading into a natural, intuitive extension of your musicianship.

Reflections

So, you're here now. You've started the journey, knowing that sight-reading is a skill worth mastering. You've likely struggled before—maybe relying on memorization, feeling stuck, or second-guessing every note. That's normal. Most musicians focus on technique and repetition while overlooking the deeper process of reflection—the key to true fluency.

This section is about building a foundation that lasts, one that strengthens not just your sight-reading but your overall musicianship. Reading, interpretation, adaptability—these skills shape how you interact with music far beyond the notes on a page. As you move forward, take time to reflect. Where do you hesitate? What patterns confuse you? Identifying these gaps will unlock new levels of control and confidence.

Progress comes from focused, intentional work. The more you refine your approach, the more natural sight-reading—and music itself—will feel.

CHAPTER ONE

Breaking Down Sight-Reading: How It Works & Why It Matters

"Your brain is faster than your hands—both the problem and the solution. When you sight-read, your eyes scan ahead, your brain deciphers symbols, your muscles respond, and your ears verify—all in fractions of a second. It's a continuous feedback loop, too fast to analyze in real time. Yet, many approach sight-reading as a slow, linear task, when in reality, it's more like piloting a jet at full speed."

Introduction

HAVE YOU EVER WONDERED how the Sight-Reading Engine Works? You've spent countless hours on new music, slowing it down ridiculously, yet it still doesn't flow. Something is messing up your engine. Without checking the blueprint, you might be patching symptoms instead of fixing the real problem. As we look under the hood, don't assume, observe. This chapter lays out the blueprint, but the full book holds the complete troubleshooting guide, even for hidden issues you didn't realize were holding you back.

Improving sight-reading starts with identifying what's working and what's not. Instead of blindly repeating the same approach, we need to evaluate, refine, and adjust. This chapter breaks down the process into essential components, revealing exactly where things break down. With a clear blueprint, you'll finally have the framework to fix inefficiencies and unlock true fluency.

To understand sight-reading, we need to reverse the domino effect—starting from success and working backward. A flawless execution means the right sound was produced. That sound came from a precise action, driven by an accurate neural command. The brain issued that command based on visual input from the score. By deconstructing this chain in reverse, we can uncover what drives fluency and, more importantly, what disrupts it.

Although these steps seem straightforward, most of the process happens subconsciously. The challenge is bringing each component into awareness and refining it until fluency feels effortless. Sight-reading works like a four-part ensemble—each section must function in sync. If one part falters, the entire system breaks down. Now, let's examine each component and fine-tune your sight-reading engine.

The Building Blocks

Sight-reading flows effortlessly when four key components work together in sync. If one weakens, the entire process slows down, making sight-reading feel clunky and unnatural.

Everything starts with visual recognition—your eyes scan ahead, absorbing notation. Instantly, the neural component assigns meaning, mapping out notes, rhythms, and phrasing. The brain sends commands to the kinetic component, activating fingers, breath, or vocal cords to bring the music to life. Finally, the auditory component steps in, providing real-time feedback on pitch, timing, and expression, closing the loop and refining execution.

These steps don't run one after another—they happen at the same time. Strong sight-readers don't think about each piece separately. Their eyes anticipate, their brain predicts, their hands move instinctively, and their ears correct instantly. Sight-Reading fluency does not come out of nowhere. It's not a miracle nor an inherited skill. It's the result of clear, structured training that builds speed, accuracy, and coordination between these four elements. Repetition alone won't get you there. Training the wrong way strengthens bad habits. Mastering sight-reading starts with understanding how these components work together, diagnosing weak spots, and refining the process until it feels effortless.

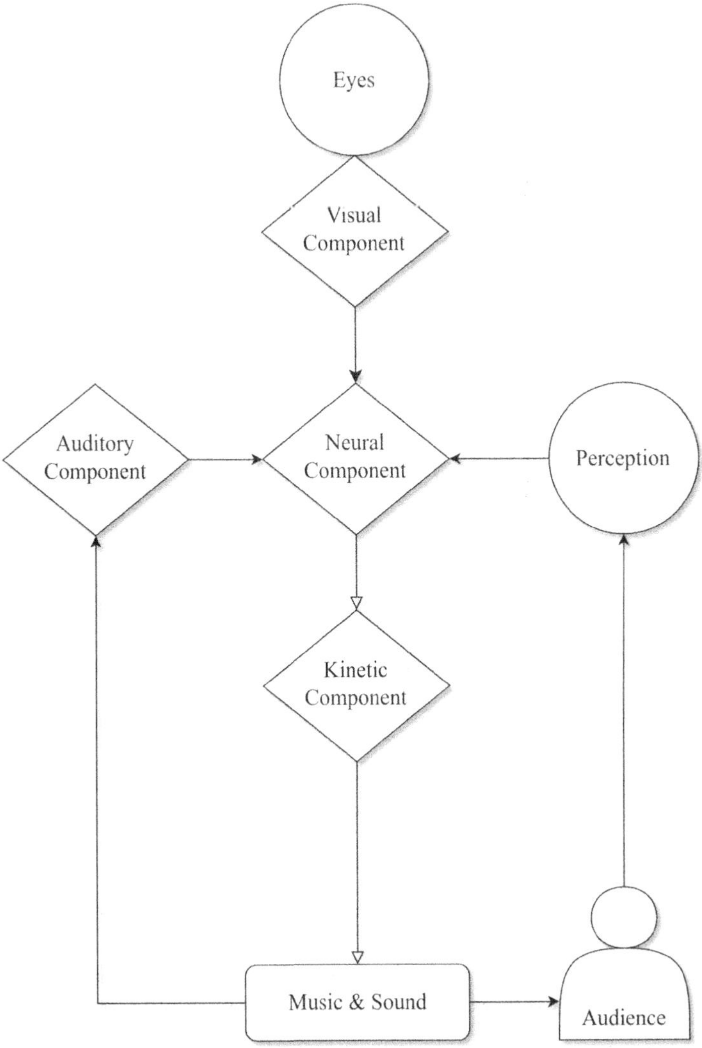

The Visual Component

Sight-reading starts with the eyes. Before a note is played, the brain processes patterns, rhythms, and structures—just like reading words. Skilled musicians don't track individual notes; they see entire phrases at a glance. Reading note by note slows you down.

To build fluency, you need to scan ahead, recognize patterns, and anticipate movement. This skill starts away from the instrument. Score Scanning (the concept at the core of section 2) and habitual sight singing drills sharpen the brain's ability to faster eye movement for note and pattern recognition. Issues in the visual component—like poor vision or sleep deprivation—compound throughout the process, creating hesitation and breaking the entire system down.

The Neural Component

Once the eyes capture notation, the brain must process and translate it into action. This is where symbols become music—where phrasing, rhythm, and expression take shape in real time. The neural component is the command center, decoding information and directing movement instantly.

If this processing slows down, hesitation creeps in. Anxiety, fatigue, or poor hydration can cloud decision-making, making even familiar passages feel unpredictable. The brain must stay sharp, assigning meaning and shaping articulation without delay.

The neural component links notation to execution. In Chapter 2, we explore how music theory strengthens this process. Later, in Section 3, we refine perception, mindset, and self-awareness—ensuring your brain operates at peak efficiency for fluid, expressive sight-reading.

The Kinetic Component

Kinetics—the coordination of movement—translates musical intent into physical execution. Sight-reading demands instant, controlled motion, where every action aligns with visual and neural processing. Precision, stamina, and technical agility must support fluency under pressure.

Even with strong visual recognition and neural processing, poor kinetic control disrupts flow. Posture, tension, and fatigue can interfere, causing unnecessary strain and reducing accuracy. Movements must be economical and automatic, allowing focus to remain on interpretation rather than mechanics.

This brain-body connection requires refinement. In Chapter 3, we explore strategies to optimize movement, develop muscle memory, and eliminate inefficiencies—ensuring technique supports expression rather than restricting it. The goal goes beyond accuracy, aiming for effortless execution that elevates musicality.

The Auditory Component

The auditory component closes the loop in sight-reading, acting as a built-in feedback system. As you play, your ear evaluates rhythm, pitch, and tone, ensuring that execution matches intent. This real-time assessment allows for instant corrections, refining phrasing, dynamics, and articulation.

When auditory processing is weak, sight-reading becomes guesswork. Simply recognizing notes and executing movements falls short— listening is the very last link in the chain-reaction reconnecting into the neural component. Hearing loss, tinnitus, or hypersensitivity to sound can generate friction or distortions, making adjustments unnecessary or even inadequate. A well-trained ear enhances confidence, adaptability, and musical intuition.

Auditory feedback detects mistakes in real time, flagging errors in pitch, rhythm, or phrasing. Without the right mindset, this disrupts flow. Chapter 7 shows how to process these signals productively, ensuring feedback refines execution instead of derailing it—keeping sight-reading smooth and adaptable.

Perception as a Silent Force in Sight-Reading

Perception drives everything in sight-reading. It goes beyond simply recognizing notes—it shapes how you interpret, respond, and adapt in the moment. In the early stages, perception tends to be reactive. A musician sight-reading during an audition or ensemble setting engages with more than just the written music; they take in the room's energy, the silence between phrases, the weight of expectations, and the subtle, unspoken cues around them. These elements do more than compete for attention—they actively shape neural processing, influencing performance just as profoundly as technique does.

With training, perception shifts from external pressure to internal control. Instead of reacting to fear or scrutiny, advanced musicians channel this "vibe" into their phrasing, structure, and flow—tailoring sight-reading to the audience for maximum impact. The key is making perception work for you, not against you. This chapter introduces perception in execution, but its deeper impact unfolds in Section 3—where mindset, self-awareness, and visualization redefine not just how you play, but how you experience music.

Hidden Obstacles

Sometimes, the problem goes beyond technique—it stems from something deeper, something hidden. Subtle factors can interfere with any of the four components, creating obstacles you may not even realize exist. While solutions—both medical and holistic—are available, identifying the issue is the first step. If something feels off, don't ignore it. Seek guidance from qualified professionals, ensuring they understand your goal: improving sight-reading as a musician. Here are some common hidden obstacles that could be holding you back.

Visual Obstacles: Poor vision, eye strain, or conditions like astigmatism can disrupt sight-reading by making it harder to process notation accurately. Lighting, screen glare, and prolonged focus on intricate details can further intensify visual fatigue, slowing recognition and increasing errors. Regular eye exams and proactive strain management keep your visual processing sharp and effortless.

Neurological Obstacles: Anxiety, ADHD, or lack of sleep can severely impact focus and slow visual processing. Over-practice and prolonged stress drain cognitive energy, reducing neural efficiency. External distractions and emotional states interfere with concentration, making it harder to stay mentally engaged during sight-reading—whether in practice or performance.

Kinetic Obstacles: Arthritis, tendonitis, and repetitive strain injuries can limit precision, endurance, and agility. Poor posture, unergonomic setups, or inefficient technique worsen these issues, leading to discomfort or long-term damage. Optimizing posture and movement reduces strain, ensuring effortless and sustainable execution.

Auditory Obstacles: Tinnitus, partial hearing loss, or hypersensitivity to sound can make it difficult to assess pitch, rhythm, and tone accurately. Background noise, certain frequencies, or sudden volume shifts may overwhelm or distort auditory feedback, making real-time adjustments less reliable. Managing sensory input and strengthening listening skills help maintain precision in musical interpretation.

Before you attempt sight reading again, take time to identify whether any of the obstacles mentioned (or others ones not mentioned) are disrupting one or more of the four components. Spotting these obstacles in your process can explain why sight reading feels more frustrating than it should. Targeted strategies can help you overcome them and unlock your full potential. While a condition may directly affect one component, its impact often spills into others. For example, astigmatism doesn't just blur notation—it strains focus, affecting neural processing. Anxiety isn't just a mental barrier—it can create muscle tension, disrupting the kinetic component, or trigger auditory hypersensitivity, making real-time feedback unreliable. Understanding these connections is key to fixing inefficiencies. By addressing the root cause, you can strengthen every aspect of your sight-reading system and perform with clarity, control, and confidence.

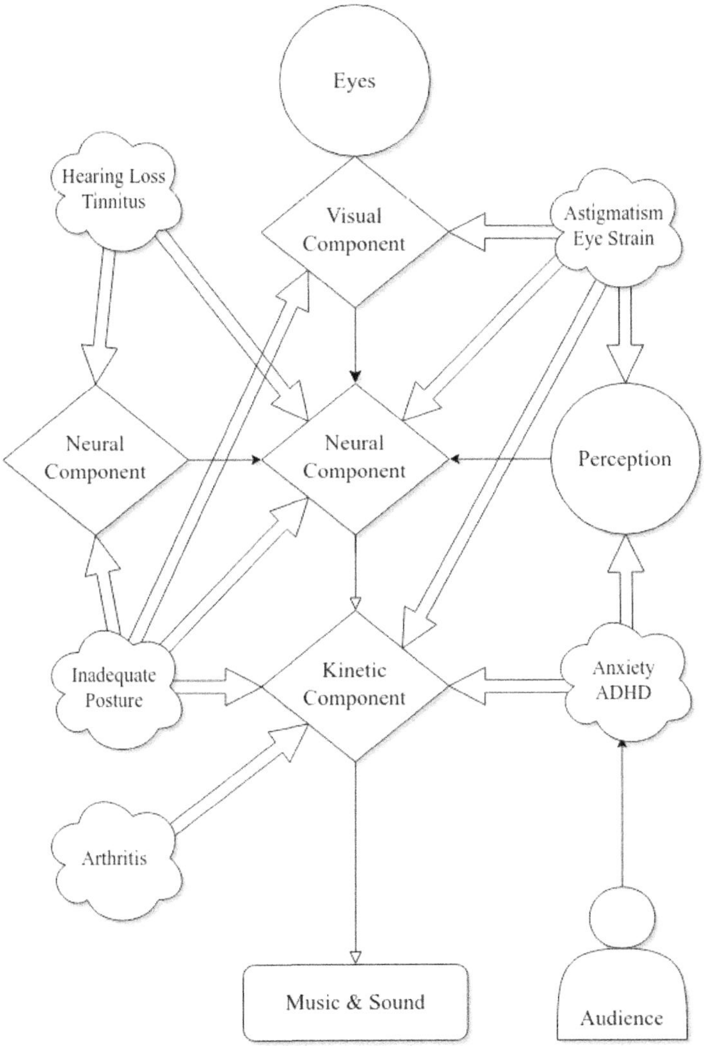

Reflections

This chapter unpacked the four essential components of sight-reading—visual, neural, kinetic, and auditory. These elements don't operate in isolation; they form a continuous feedback loop, each influencing the others. When one weakens, the entire system breaks flow. Recognizing these connections is key to shifting sight-reading from frustration to fluency.

Many musicians unknowingly overdevelop one area while neglecting another—sharp aural skills but slow hands, strong technique but weak pattern recognition. Awareness of these imbalances is the first step toward fixing them.

Ultimately, sight-reading fluency means navigating difficulty instinctively instead of avoiding it. When the four components stop competing for attention and start working as a unified system, music flows effortlessly. Each refined movement, each recognized pattern, each note processed with intention moves you closer to effortless execution. In the next chapter, we go deeper—exploring the intellectual tools that shape interpretation. Theory, historical context, and phrasing don't just color sight-reading; they turn it into an art.

CHAPTER TWO

KNOWLEDGE OF MUSIC THEORY AND HISTORY

"What if I told you sight-reading isn't just about notes—it's about memory? Not just muscle memory, but the memory of centuries of music theory and history living inside your brain. The faster you recall these patterns, the faster you sight-read. Let's unlock that memory."

Introduction

IN CHAPTER 1, WE laid out the blueprint of the sight-reading engine and its four components. But even the best engine needs proper filtration to run efficiently. Chapter 2 examines the filters of the neural component: music theory and music history—regulating the flow of information to refine interpretation and shape a personalized, expressive musical voice. Proper integration allows the brain to process only what enhances clarity, ensuring a smooth and expressive musical flow.

Knowing a composer's style and historical context provides a level of predictability in sight-reading. Harmonic progressions, phrase structures, and cadential patterns often follow established conventions, allowing musicians to anticipate musical direction. The score then acts as validation, confirming those expectations and guiding execution with confidence.

Without this knowledge, sight-reading becomes a note-by-note struggle, forcing constant micro-decisions that slow down processing. Instead of reading fluently, the brain gets stuck deciphering each detail in isolation, making real-time execution far more difficult. Educated anticipation removes this obstacle, allowing for a faster, more natural interpretation.

Music theory sharpens perception, turning notes into structure and chaos into clarity. It allows you to anticipate chord progressions, recognize melodic patterns, and understand harmonic function instantly. Sight-reading without theory is like reading words without grammar—you might pronounce them, but their meaning remains unclear.

Music history brings depth and expression to sight-reading. It's not just about recognizing a Baroque dance; it's about feeling its pulse and shaping articulation accordingly. A Romantic melody goes beyond a simple sequence of notes—it becomes a flowing narrative.Knowing when to stretch time, where to breathe, and how to shape a phrase elevates the music beyond notation, turning execution into an active, intentional, and immersive experience for the listener.

This chapter will inspire you to rewire your brain, embedding theory and history until they become instinct. When these elements are fully internalized, sight-reading stops being mere decoding and becomes instinct. You won't need extra time to prepare—you'll need a faster brain, one that instantly retrieves centuries of musical knowledge. By the end of this chapter, you'll understand why sight-reading without theory and history becomes not only more difficult, but nearly impossible to do well.

Artificial vs. Human

At the end of the 20th century, MIDI (Musical Instrument Digital Interface) revolutionized digital music production, enabling computers and synthesizers to reproduce notation with flawless timing, pitch, and articulation. While groundbreaking, MIDI remains inherently limited—it is programmed, not performed. Even with advancements in sample-based MIDI libraries, where real instrument sounds are recorded and played back, the result is still an imitation. No matter how high-quality the samples, they lack the organic nuance of live performance. The subtle imperfections, the spontaneous adjustments, and the expressive intent that make music feel alive are absent. No two human performances are ever truly identical, yet MIDI will repeat itself endlessly—without growth, without struggle, and without soul.

But now, we have artificial intelligence. Unlike MIDI, which is merely playback, AI can compose, analyze, and even "perform" music. Trained on centuries of compositions, AI can instantly access vast databases of recordings, interpretations, theoretical frameworks, historical contexts, and stylistic nuances. It can recognize a fugue and construct one, apply harmonies with precision, and even mimic a performer's phrasing. In the near future, robots may physically play real instruments, eliminating the limitations of sampled sound and bringing machine performance closer to human execution. Yet, despite this progress, one thing remains beyond AI's reach—the raw, personal experience that fuels human artistry.

Yet even then, AI lacks the one thing that gives music its soul: humanity. It does not struggle, wrestle with doubt, or push through fatigue in pursuit of expression. It does not feel loss, love, or longing. AI can replicate every note of Chopin with flawless precision, but it will never understand why he wrote them.

And here lies a crucial lesson: MIDI and AI aren't threats—they are benchmarks. They raise the bar, proving that we, as human musicians, have no excuse to let them outpace us in knowledge and execution. AI can access theoretical and historical data instantaneously, but instead of being discouraged, we should take that as a challenge. AI doesn't make musicians irrelevant—it exposes what we need to refine. If a machine can recall harmonic functions and stylistic traits in an instant, why shouldn't we train our minds to do the same? The faster we internalize theory and history, the more instinctive and fluid our sight-reading becomes. Technology doesn't replace us—it reminds us to evolve.

MIDI teaches us precision—its accuracy in note execution should inspire us to master the kinetic component of playing, which will be explored in Chapter 3. AI teaches us instant recall—its database-driven approach reminds us that the best sight-readers don't merely react, they anticipate. A musician with a deep theoretical and historical foundation can read ahead, recognize patterns, and interpret before the hands even touch the instrument.

Unlike AI, we have a unique personalized interpretation style. There's a sense of identity, uniqueness, and pride. But there's also emotion—hesitation, missteps, even moments of irrationality. Sometimes, what feels like a mistake in the moment later reveals itself as brilliance—a spontaneous decision that transforms the performance into something unforgettable. A machine will never take risks in performance because it has nothing to risk. That vulnerability—that raw, human unpredictability—is what makes music real. Technology is an incredible tool, but it remains just that—a tool. It does not replace artistry. The best musicians won't compete with machines for perfection; they will embrace what AI can never replicate: the human act of turning ink on a page into something alive. In sight-reading, we must merge the best of both worlds—the precision of MIDI, the speed of AI, and the irreplaceable soul of human expression. A machine will never feel the weight of a crescendo or the quiet ache of a resolved dissonance. That's our gift. And no AI, no robot, no digital playback will ever take that away.

Music Theory

Nothing accelerates sight-reading like a deep understanding of music theory. Your goal is to process entire phrases, recognize harmonic functions at a glance, and anticipate resolutions before they happen. Theory transforms note reading into idea recognition, eliminating hesitation and replacing it with confirmation.

Without theory, sight-reading becomes guesswork. A modulation feels like an abrupt, unexplained shift rather than a natural transition. Musicians without a strong theoretical foundation are forced to read everything at face value, working harder for a fraction of the results. Those who understand theory see patterns instead of problems, allowing them to focus on phrasing, expression, and interpretation rather than mere execution.

When a musician can instinctively recognize cadences, secondary dominants, and harmonic functions, the brain begins to predict rather than simply react. This shift allows music to unfold, transforming sight-reading from a mechanical exercise into an intuitive, expressive act.

Music theory is often misunderstood as an academic pursuit separate from real-world musical application, but in truth, it is a shortcut to instant musical comprehension. The deeper a musician internalizes harmony, form, and voice leading, the faster they can decode, interpret, and perform any piece of music effortlessly. By training the mind to recognize patterns, resolutions, and harmonic tendencies, sight-reading becomes fluid rather than rigid, allowing a musician to process and execute complex music without hesitation. The following are only broad examples—music theory extends far beyond what is mentioned here. There are numerous resources to explore these concepts in greater depth, including focused material available in our complimentary extra resources.

Form and Structure – Recognizing form and structure helps musicians anticipate transitions, recurring themes, and sectional changes.

Texture and Layering – Recognizing texture and motion helps balance voices and maintain clarity, especially in ensembles.

Harmonic Functions – Mastering harmonic functions helps navigate movement and anticipate resolutions in tonic, dominant, and chromatic harmonies.

Modulation and Cadences – Recognizing key changes and cadences early ensures smoother transitions, clearer phrasing, and structural awareness.

Phrase Structure – Identifying phrases, sequences, and motivic repetition helps shape musical expression and structural clarity.

Counterpoint – Identifying counterpoint clarifies how independent melodic lines interact, ensuring balance in complex textures.

Voice Leading – Voice motion predicts note movement, enhancing continuity while reducing uncertainty and errors.

Rhythm and Meter – Understanding subdivisions and time signatures improves interpretation, rhythmic precision, and overall execution in performance.

Syncopation – Understanding syncopation ensures rhythmic stability and allows musicians to execute off-beat phrasing naturally.

Polyrhythm – Polyrhythms demand multi-layered rhythmic awareness and a strong internal pulse for precise execution.

Harmonic Rhythm – Harmonic rhythm shapes phrasing and motion; understanding its pace prevents misinterpretation of musical flow.

While these theoretical concepts are original to classical music, they can be just as important in other styles, particularly jazz due to its harmonic and rhythmic complexity. Thus, while music theory is non-negotiable for classical musicians, it can be an invaluable tool for musicians of any genre. Music theory, when deeply internalized, dissolves complexity, making sight-reading not just possible, but instinctive. Treat it as your ultimate advantage—a tool that lets you read ahead, interpret instantly, and turn every new score into an opportunity for expressive, confident performance.

Music History

Sight-reading certainly benefits from a strong understanding of historical context. Stylistic awareness shapes phrasing, articulation, and interpretation, allowing musicians to read fluently and accurately without second-guessing. However, those examples below are mere broad strokes on the canvas—there are many resources available to explore these periods in depth, including laser focused material in our complimentary extra resources.

Renaissance (1400–1600) – Polyphony defines the era, with smooth voice leading, imitative counterpoint, and modal harmonies. Phrasing follows the natural flow of vocal lines, requiring clear articulation and balanced textures. Instruments often mimic vocal phrasing, making legato playing essential.

Baroque (1600–1750) – Ornamentation, figured bass, and dance-inspired rhythms create contrast and motion. Harmonic progressions are driven by sequences and suspensions, with clear tonal direction. Sight-reading demands fluency in embellishments, rhythmic precision, and articulation that highlights dynamic contrasts.

Classical (1750–1820) – Clarity, balance, and symmetry shape the phrasing. Sonata form structures much of the repertoire, requiring awareness of harmonic movement and motivic development. Sight-reading relies on recognizing phrase patterns, controlled dynamics, and the elegance of proportionate articulation.

Romantic (1820–1900) – Expansive melodies, chromaticism, and expressive flexibility define the style. Rubato influences phrasing, demanding an intuitive sense of timing. Harmonic tension and shifting textures require adaptability, with a focus on dynamic contrast and lyrical expression.

These stylistic foundations extend beyond classical music. Understanding a composer's influences and a genre's evolution refines interpretation. This strong pursuit of knowledge benefits performers across all styles, genres, and time periods. Exploring a piece's origins reveals insights that elevate performance from competent to compelling.

Visual into Neural

It's obvious that your brain and eyes constantly work together, refining what you see in real time. The optic nerve isn't just a one-way data stream—it works both ways, filtering perception through experience and knowledge. A trained musician prepares and knows where to look. Educated anticipation fine-tunes both the kinetic and visual components, making sight-reading faster and more intuitive.

Yet, the relationship between the neural and visual components is often overlooked. Think about it—you train your technique, your hands, your coordination... but are you training your eyes? Your fingers respond to what your brain tells them, but your brain can only process what your eyes deliver. If sight-reading relies on how efficiently you process notation, then eye training and its coordination with the neural component should be just as much a priority as technical mastery.

When reading words, you don't process each letter in isolation—you instantly recognize whole words and their meaning. You don't see C-A-T as three separate letters; you see "cat," an animal. But it goes even further. Take the word COOL for example. Depending on context and intention, it could be used to describe temperature OR serve as a cultural slang showcasing social approval. The same word can have vastly different meanings, shaped by how the author intends them and how the reader interprets them. Music works the same way. Mature sight-readers see the meaning in the patterns, phrases, harmonic structures. They recognize a cadence as a resolution, not just isolated chords. The question is: have you trained your brain to see music this way? If you're still reading note by note, it's like trying to read a book by spelling out every word. Sight-reading fluency begins when your brain stops processing music as isolated data and starts recognizing it as a structured language.

The same happens for patterns, harmonies, scales, and sequences—they shouldn't be read in isolation. Educated anticipation prepares the mind for their occurrence before they appear, accelerating decision-making and enhancing phrasing. Through subconscious repetition, these elements become second nature, ensuring a seamless connection between the Visual and Neural components, allowing sight-reading to flow effortlessly rather than being pieced together note by note.

The key is training the brain to filter visual input efficiently. Instead of processing individual notes, sight-readers must recognize harmonic movement, melodic contour, and structural form to reduce hesitation and enhance expressiveness. Adding historical awareness transforms sight-reading from decoding the unknown to reading a familiar story. Musicians who develop this skill can now confidently predict and adapt while sight-reading, making every score feel intuitive rather than unpredictable.

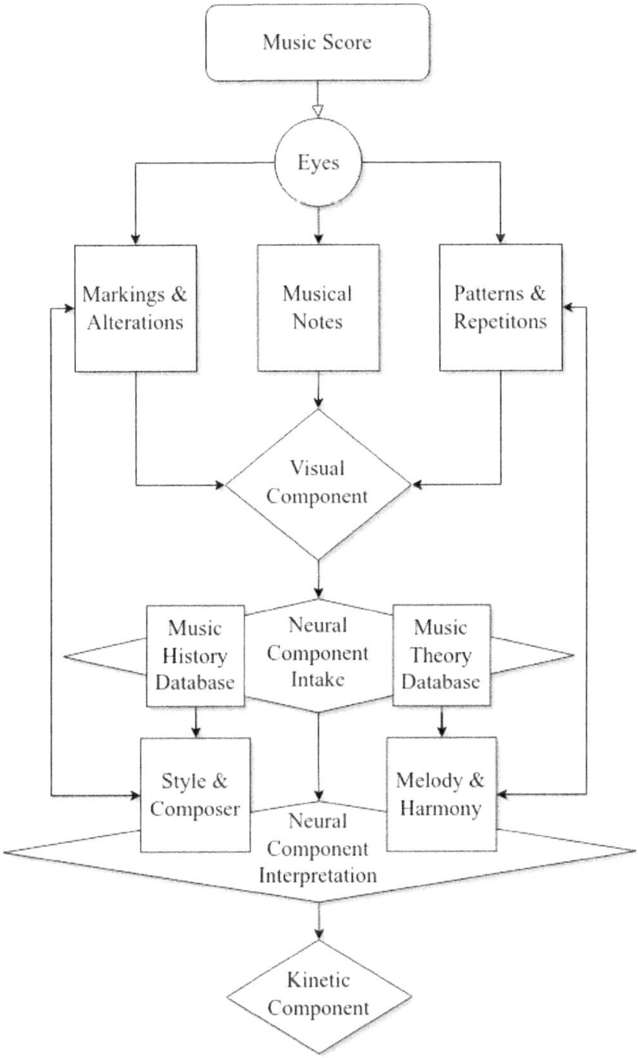

Reflections

By integrating theory and history, you've turned sight-reading from a mechanical task into a musical conversation. Notes are no longer just symbols—they carry meaning, structure, and intention. Mastering these tools allows you to anticipate patterns, hear harmonic direction before it unfolds, and interpret music instinctively.

Music theory sharpens awareness. Recognizing key signatures, time signatures, harmonic structures, and form lets the brain process music in meaningful chunks, not isolated notes. A ii-V-I progression or a fugue subject isn't just something to be read—it's something to expect. The deeper these concepts are embedded, the more effortlessly they guide interpretation. Patterns emerge naturally, and reading becomes an educated prediction rather than a mere reaction.

Historical awareness refines expression. Understanding a composer's era shapes phrasing, articulation, and stylistic choices. A Baroque dance demands crisp articulation, while a Romantic nocturne calls for fluid rubato. Listening to great interpreters strengthens this instinct, helping you internalize stylistic nuances that elevate both sight-reading and musicianship.

Yet, knowledge alone will only take you so far. True mastery demands action. Understanding theory, recognizing historical contexts, and developing fluency through diverse exposure form the foundation—but without deliberate, consistent practice, these insights remain dormant.

Chapter 3 explores the transformative power of turning insight into practice, theory into technique, and potential into performance. It's not enough to know; it's imperative to put it into action.

CHAPTER THREE

MASTERING YOUR INSTRUMENT WITH PRECISION & CONTROL

"Knowing how to run isn't the same as running. You can study form and mechanics, but until your feet hit the ground, it's just theory. Sight-reading is no different. Recognizing notes and patterns means nothing if your hands can't keep up. The gap between knowledge and execution isn't closed by more thinking—it's closed by movement, precision, and control."

Introduction

IN CHAPTER 2, WE explored how the visual and neural components work together, using music theory and history to decode and interpret the score. But intellectual interpretation alone falls short—music comes alive through execution. Now, in Chapter 3, we shift from thought to action. The kinetic component is where the brain's commands become movement, where technique meets artistry, and where true sight-reading fluency is either achieved—or broken. For execution to match vision, the transition from neural to kinetic must be seamless, precise, and instinctive. This is where muscle memory, coordination, and control determine whether sight-reading flows effortlessly or falls apart under pressure.

Without control, even the best interpretation falls apart. Your technique must bridge the gap between vision and execution, transforming notes into expression with precision and ease. As you sharpen your awareness of key technical skills, posture, muscle coordination, articulation, and touch take on new importance. These aren't just details; they are the mechanics of fluency. Train them, refine them, and your instrument becomes an extension of your musical intent. Ignore them, and every passage becomes a fight against hesitation. By refining these elements, you ensure that your body moves as fast as your mind, allowing you to sight-read with confidence, control, and artistry.

Building technical skill is one of the most demanding yet deeply rewarding aspects of musicianship. True mastery goes beyond mechanics—it's about developing a complete connection with your instrument physically, emotionally, and conceptually. It means knowing how to produce the sound you envision while maintaining balance, efficiency, and control. This connection goes far beyond technique; it requires patience, dedication, and a lifelong pursuit of refinement, where every improvement brings you closer to effortless expression.

Neural to Kinetic

The neural and kinetic components form a feedback loop where mental processing and physical execution work in sync. Just as the brain interprets notation, the body must respond with precision and control. If this connection is weak, sight-reading becomes clumsy and inefficient. The brain anticipates movement, while the body delivers it without hesitation. This is why technical fluency is crucial: if the hands struggle to keep up, sight-reading falls apart.

Much like the visual and neural connection, this process is not one-directional. The brain instructs movement, but the body provides feedback—posture, tension, and technique directly impact how easily notes are executed. Poor positioning or excess tension creates resistance, slowing reaction time and introducing errors. A musician with strong neural-kinetic coordination moves with efficiency, adjusting on the fly and responding to technical demands in real time. In this chapter, we focus on the physics of the instrument, posture, and physical well-being, refining the ergonomic foundation that allows sight-reading to flow. By aligning technical control with artistic intent, you build a fluid, instinctive connection between thought and action—ensuring that what you read is not just understood, but executed effortlessly.

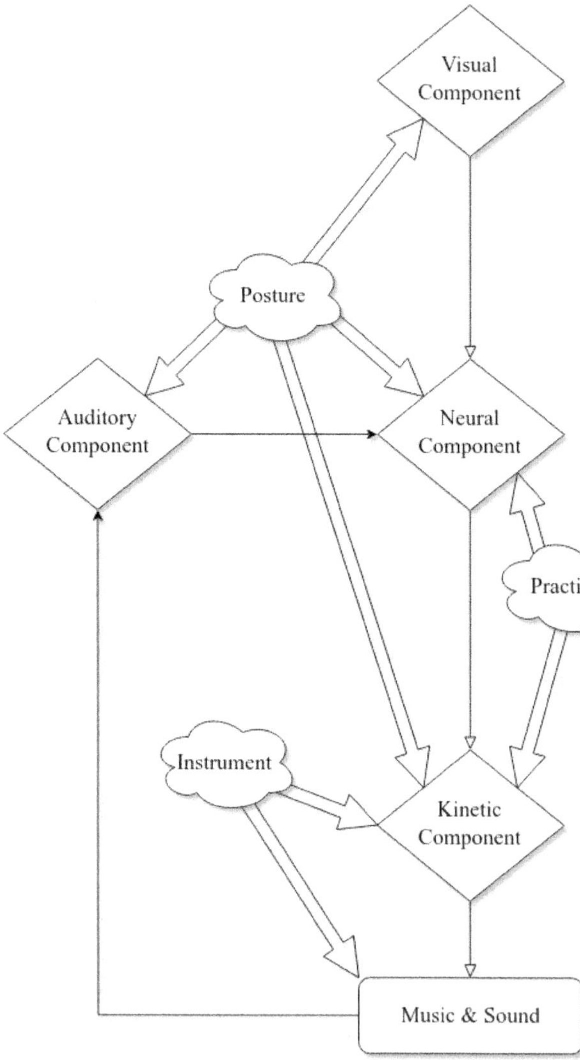

Factor 1 – The Physics

Every instrument operates on its own physical principles, shaping how sound is generated, controlled, and projected.

Mastering sight-reading goes far beyond recognizing notes—it requires understanding how your instrument responds to your actions. This knowledge must be practical. Knowing what your instrument is made of means little unless it impacts how you play. The real value lies in understanding how physical factors influence execution, allowing you to adapt, refine, and optimize technique based on how the instrument behaves.

A good mentor can guide your technique, but deeper fluency comes from direct experience—feeling how your instrument reacts under different conditions and making adjustments in real time. The right awareness eliminates technical inefficiencies, preventing struggle and hesitation. Instead of working against your instrument, you learn to work with it, making movement more efficient, controlled, and expressive. Mastery often develops gradually, as your understanding of the instrument begins to inform subtle choices in technique, allowing expression and control to grow together over time.

For a deeper understanding of your instrument, detailed individual instrument sheets are available in the extended complimentary content. These resources break down key physical and mechanical aspects, ensuring that this knowledge is practical and applicable to your playing. You'll find the access code at the end of this book.

Factor 2 – The Musician's Body

Posture is where technique begins and mastery is either built or broken. It determines how efficiently your body interacts with your instrument, directly affecting precision, control, and longevity. Poor posture leads to tension, instability, and injury—turning even simple passages into a struggle. Proper alignment ensures that movement is fluid, muscles work efficiently, and every note is executed with ease.

Every instrument has a unique set of physical demands, but the principles of posture remain universal. Whether you bow, pluck, press, or breathe, your posture defines how easily you execute movement. You should never fight against your instrument—instead, your setup should allow for effortless execution that supports both technical accuracy and expressive freedom. Musicians often overlook posture until pain, fatigue, or technical limitations force them to address it. This reactive approach slows progress. Fixing bad habits is harder than building good ones from the start. The earlier you refine your posture, the sooner it becomes second nature—reducing strain, improving endurance, and reinforcing fluid technique.

Beyond posture, many factors influence the musician's body, from flexibility and strength to endurance and recovery. Chapter 8 explores these elements in depth, providing strategies to maintain long-term physical health. But here, we focus on the foundation—posture. Without it, even the best technical approach can collapse under pressure. Some adjustments yield immediate improvements; others require consistent refinement. Knowing when to make quick corrections and when to commit to gradual change is key to effective practice. Posture is both an instant fix and a long-term investment. Get it right, and your body becomes an extension of your musical intent—capable, responsive, and free from unnecessary tension.

Factor 3 – Practice

Practice is where everything comes together. It's the bridge between knowledge and execution, awareness and instinct, thought and action. This is where the neural, kinetic, and instrumental elements sync, forging the subconscious fluency required for effortless sight-reading. True mastery means transitioning from conscious effort to automatic response. Every technical refinement, every movement fine-tuned in practice, must evolve from deliberate control into subconscious competence. The goal is not just to play—it's to react instinctively, allowing the hands to execute without hesitation while the mind stays ahead.

This process begins with posture, ensuring that movement is natural, efficient, and free from tension. From there, practice sharpens tone, precision, and muscle memory—the elements that determine how fluidly your body interacts with the instrument. Repeating scales, positions, and intervals with focused intent develops an instinctive kinetic response, preparing your hands to move as fast as your brain processes notation.

Effective practice involves more than repetition—it requires mindful refinement. Without awareness, high volume can reinforce bad habits; without consistency, even focused work may lose momentum. Progress depends on both elements supporting each other. Each session should gradually improve efficiency, control, and adaptability, addressing potential issues before they affect performance. It also helps to maintain a respectful relationship with your instrument. Things like worn strings, poor tuning, or neglect can quietly add resistance, making it harder to align intention with execution. A well-maintained instrument supports smoother progress and helps keep practice focused and productive.

Ultimately, practice serves not only to prepare but to transform. As the connection between thought and movement becomes more refined, performance demands less conscious effort. Sight-reading fluency starts to take shape when execution feels natural, allowing the music to unfold with clarity and ease, free from interruption or resistance.

Prompts for Self-Assessment:

Instrument Knowledge: Can you identify and explain how your instrument produces sound? Do you understand how materials, construction, and maintenance affect its performance? Task: Research one aspect of your instrument's construction (e.g., strings, keys, or valves) and experiment with how it affects your playing.

Posture and Body Awareness: Are you playing in a way that aligns with your body's natural movements? Do you experience tension, discomfort, or fatigue during or after practice? Video Record yourself playing for 5 minutes playing memorized music and 5 minutes sight-reading music. Analyze your posture and identify areas of tension. Discuss findings with a mentor or physical specialist.

Practice Routine: Is your practice focused and intentional, addressing posture, tone, and muscle memory? Are you varying your practice to build versatility, or repeating the same routines without growth? Create a weekly practice schedule that includes exercises for tone, scales, and sight-reading. Dedicate time to address specific challenges.

Instrument Maintenance: Is your instrument in optimal condition? Are you regularly tuning, cleaning, or replacing parts as needed? Perform a maintenance check on your instrument. If unsure how, consult a professional or watch an instructional video.

Reflections

The ultimate goal of mastering your instrument is to build sustainable habits that enable consistent, high-quality performance. This is especially critical for sight-reading, where you must transform written notation into sound instantly and effectively. Your instrument must become an extension of your body and mind, ready to deliver the exact timbres, dynamics, and articulations you envision. Achieving this level of fluency requires constant refinement of the three foundational elements outlined in this chapter: understanding your instrument's physics, maintaining a healthy posture, and practicing intentionally.

Beyond technical mastery, a musician's relationship with their instrument is deeply personal. The more intimately you understand its sound, mechanics, and response, the more naturally it will become an extension of your artistic voice. However absolute mastery of your instrument will never be achieved. Mastery is a lifelong path with your instrument seeking a deeper expression and connection.

Every musician's journey is unique, and progress depends on consistent self-assessment and adjustment. Each of the three factors—physics, posture, and practice—will evolve over time as you grow as a musician. Regularly revisiting these concepts ensures that your foundation remains strong and adaptable, preventing bad habits from taking root. Shortcuts may seem tempting, but mastery demands patience, focus, and a willingness to invest time and effort.

Mastery is a lifelong pursuit. The way you train your hands, posture, and breath shapes not just your playing, but your ability to translate notes into effortless sound. Every refined technique, every intentional movement brings you closer to fluency.

Now, you have the foundation. You've explored the core components of sight-reading, the historical and theoretical context that shapes interpretation, and the technical skills that support confident execution. Yet even with all this knowledge, something critical must still be done in the moments before you strike the first note. In Section 2, we'll explore the essential pre-sightreading habits that prime your mind, body, and instincts before a single sound is made. Because mature sight-readers don't react to the music—they set themselves up to control it from the moment they open the score.

SECTION TWO

Adopting Discipline Through Productive Habits

Introduction

Imagine you're in a rehearsal with a new group, a brand-new score on your stand. You start playing—but eight measures in, you're lost. Distracted, struggling to catch up, mistake after mistake. You know you could play this piece if it were memorized, yet here you are, unprepared for the reality of sight-reading. How many more times will this happen?

Section I gave you the tools to understand how sight-reading works—how your visual, neural, kinetic, and auditory systems interact. You refined your technique, strengthened your posture, and deepened your knowledge of music theory and history. By all accounts, you should have been ready—yet you still struggled to deliver a strong first reading. So what went wrong? Think of Section I as your left leg—strong but limited on its own. To walk, you need both legs alternating their work. This section provides that missing balance, control, and endurance, ensuring that your sight-reading becomes fluid, natural, and reliable in any setting.

The habit you'll build here is simple but requires consistency—like brushing your teeth. Skip it, and decay sets in. The same applies to sight-reading: neglect preparation, and bad habits take root. But when done correctly and consistently, the benefits are undeniable. This section will give you the missing piece, reinforcing your foundation and ensuring lasting progress. Master this habit, and sight-reading will become a skill you trust, not fear.

Musical Maturity

Early on, musicians don't realize that their approach, though flawed, is a necessary part of learning. We touched on this in Chapter 2, but now it's time to go deeper. Think of a child learning how to read words—slowly, they separate each letter, struggling to piece them together. "C... A... T..." they say, only realizing what they've read after they've sounded out every individual letter. Most musicians stay stuck in this stage—playing one note at a time, only realizing too late how beautiful the phrase could have been.

An adult reads differently. They don't process each letter separately—they anticipate structure, recognize patterns, and let the words flow naturally. If reading aloud, they take a moment to prepare. They glance over the length, note paragraph breaks, gather context, and decide on the appropriate tone and pacing before beginning. This quick assessment ensures clarity and expression, making the reading smooth and intentional rather than hesitant or mechanical.

That is how a mature musician should sight-read. Instead of blindly playing and hoping to understand later, they should scan the score the way an adult reads paragraphs—absorbing structure, recognizing patterns, and preparing for challenges. Which type of musician do you want to be? Will you struggle through each note like a child sounding out words, or will you approach the music with intention, shaping phrases and dynamics from the very first note, playing with confidence and control?

Preparation is the solution. You must adopt the same mindset, maturity, and framework as someone reading a passage aloud for the first time—scanning ahead, understanding structure, and setting the right tone before speaking a single word. Sight-reading should be no different. Think of Section I as your education—where you learned the alphabet, grammar, and the importance of reading fluently. But education alone was never enough. Plenty of people know how to read yet struggle to deliver a speech with clarity and conviction. That is the maturity and framework we are aiming for. A skilled speaker doesn't just read—they interpret, anticipate, and command the text, ensuring every word is delivered with purpose.

That same mindset applies here. This section is about you adopting that mature mindset: a shift from reacting to controlling, from guessing to knowing. It's about training your brain to be prepared for the music ahead of time, so that when you play, everything flows with confidence and precision. Without a doubt, sight-reading requires talent. But without preparation strategy, and intent, talent alone will not suffice.

Score Scanning

Approaching a new score should feel like entering a conversation, not getting lost in a maze. Just as a skilled speaker scans their notes before speaking, a musician should preview the score before playing. Preparation clarifies intent—and scanning is the first step. This shouldn't be a through read-through. It should be a quick, strategic habit that transforms your sight-reading for the better. In a simplified version of the world, music moves in two dimensions—horizontally through time and vertically through pitch. To navigate both, we need two types of scans. Given the complexity of each dimension, each scan is layered, ensuring all essential elements are at least acknowledged.

Horizontal Framework: Think of the horizontal scan like checking a map before a drive. You don't memorize every turn, but you note key intersections, the overall route, and estimated travel time. In music, this means scanning the time related elements such as tempo shifts and rhythmic patterns. Knowing the general path before starting is the beginning of the journey before getting in the car. You will have an idea where the music slows, where it accelerates, and how long the journey will take.

Vertical Framework: If the horizontal scan maps the route, the vertical scan reveals the terrain—the landscape that shapes the experience. Is this a smooth highway, a winding mountain road, or a rugged off-road trek? In music, this means scanning for harmonic depth, textures, melodies, and tonal shifts. Will the journey be light and open or dense and intense? Are there sudden drops or moments to soar? A well executed vertical scan helps you anticipate tensions, resolutions, and emotional color, ensuring you understand not just where the music is going, but how it will feel along the way.

Tempo, Expression, & Character

Now that you know where you're going and what kind of terrain lies ahead, it's time to decide how you'll get there. Are you taking a slow, reflective walk through a quiet town, or are you navigating a fast-moving highway, weaving through traffic? Is this a lonely road, a joyful parade, or a heavy funeral march? Your tempo sets the pace of the journey, but it also defines its meaning.

And what about your vehicle? A bicycle can zip through traffic where a car gets stuck, but would struggle on a steep mountain pass. A bus carries many passengers—you may need to match the pace of others if you're playing in an ensemble. If the road ahead is unpredictable, you need to anticipate sharp turns, sudden stops, or dangerous curves. A reckless speed can lead to collisions with tricky passages, while an overly cautious pace can drain the life from the music.

Reflections

Most musicians, when it comes to sight-reading, never step out of childhood into adulthood. They may be skilled performers who memorize music, but they still need to outgrow the habit of reading note by note. They struggle with new scores and believe that sight-reading is just a battle to endure. But from this moment on, that changes for you. The next three chapters will transform how you will adequately prepare for sight-reading before even play the first note.

Now, build the habit. Read the next three chapters and scan every score you touch, even the ones you already know. You'll be surprised by how much more there is to see—details you overlooked, patterns you never noticed, and structure that suddenly makes sense. The more you scan, the sharper your instincts will become. Make a promise to yourself: From this point on, scanning comes first and it will be a non-negotiable habit. Whether it's a familiar piece or something entirely new, commit to scanning before playing, no exceptions.

Extended Complimentary Resources Reminder

Before you continue, scan the QR code to access your complimentary resources. These include instrument-specific bootcamps for piano, guitar, flute, cello, harp, violin, and many other instruments. Each one is designed to help you apply what you're about to learn in Chapters 4, 5, and 6. You will also find sample score scans that show exactly how to execute the new techniques, along with pre-sight-reading checklists that remove guesswork and expose hidden habits holding you back. This is how you make progress: by training with methodical, scientific precision and eliminating the mistakes before you allow them to form. Use these tools daily, and your sight-reading will start to improve faster than you thought possible.

CHAPTER FOUR

The Horizontal Perspective of Music

"Digging your grave. That's exactly what you're doing every time you sight-read without scanning the score. You are shoveling dirt over your own potential and you don't even realize it. Every reckless read-through hard-wires hesitation, panic, and failure into your playing. Your bad habits aren't just sticking—they're multiplying, poisoning your talent and sabotaging your future. You might think you're getting better but you're only sealing your fate. You'll either start scanning the score, or you'll keep drowning. The choice is yours."

Introduction

The horizontal dimension of music—how it unfolds over time—plays a crucial role in shaping your ability to process information efficiently, anticipate transitions, and approach sight-reading with greater confidence. When this framework is missing, each new piece can feel disorienting and unpredictable. But as you train your brain to recognize form, structure, and recurring patterns, your relationship with the score begins to shift—from passive reaction to active control.

Horizontal Score Scanning helps build a mental processing framework that supports the ability to absorb, categorize, and anticipate musical structures. Each time you scan a score, your brain becomes more attuned to patterns, gradually making sight-reading feel more fluid. This approach is grounded in neuroscience—through consistent use, your brain becomes increasingly efficient at recognizing key information and translating it into faster, more confident execution.

Horizontal Framework Development is the process of layering the time-related information of the score into clear, actionable ideas at the outset of your reading. Instead of passively processing notes, you scan to identify tempo, rhythm, and form as interconnected components of a system. This method drastically reduces hesitation, eliminates guesswork, and makes every new piece feel familiar—even when it's completely unfamiliar. Vertical Scanning depends on this foundation—without a defined sense of time, analyzing harmony and note groupings loses its effectiveness. Prioritizing the time-based elements is essential to building a functional framework.

The goal of Horizontal Framework Development is to establish the right tempo for sight-reading. The true decision on tempo is never instant; it requires context, balance, and interpretation, which is why it must be the first thing you notice, but the last thing you finalize. Chapter 6 is dedicated entirely to choosing the right tempo but it cannot be done properly without the horizontal framework.

Time Signature and Tempo Indications

The first scan should focus on time signatures and tempo indications—the silent forces that dictate how the music moves, breathes, and unfolds before the key signature even appears. This is the foundation of Horizontal Framework Development. Without it, you step into the music with no sense of direction.

A time signature sets the rules for bar structure, tempo notation, internal logic, and natural pulse. Indeed, it is simple but absolutely critical. This scan should take seconds. Time signatures are highly visible, yet failing to acknowledge them—even with a penciled circle—invites avoidable surprises. Overlooking them undermines the purpose of building a solid horizontal framework and becomes a fundamental error. For example, in simple meters, beats group naturally in twos or fours, making notation predictable. A change of meter (for one or many bars) is also a possibility on a score and could be used to showcase your talent with adequate interpretation. Last but not least are repetitions with jumps to different sections of the score. Our goal is to avoid those surprises by marking them with a pencil and mentally integrating them as part of the horizontal framework.

The same principle applies to tempo markings like accelerandos, fermatas, ritardandos, and similar indications. These are not just instructions—they help define the music's identity and will later inform the tempo you choose to perform the piece. Unlike time signatures, they may not always require a penciled marking, but making a mental note can be beneficial in shaping your overall horizontal framework. The few seconds this scan requires are insignificant compared to the immense benefits it provides.

Rhythmic Elements

The rhythmic structure is the heartbeat of a composition, and uncovering its patterns is the goal of the second horizontal scan in Horizontal Framework Development. This scan reveals two essential rhythmic layers—the pattern within a single measure and the larger rhythmic flow that spans multiple measures. Identifying both allows you to anticipate motion, phrasing, and accents, reinforcing a stable rhythmic foundation before you play.

It should be very easy to identify the rhythmic patterns within a single measure. Use this scan to internalize the rhythmic flow ahead of playing. At this stage, no markings are typically needed, as the goal is to grasp the natural groove of the piece. These micro-patterns influence phrasing, articulation, and stability, helping you establish a clear sense of pulse before progressing to larger rhythmic structures.

However, we still have to identify rhythmic patterns that span multiple bars. This will reveal sequences, recurring motifs, and groupings that shape the larger flow of the music. Those findings might be worth circling for reference while sight-reading. Recognizing these broader rhythmic structures allows for smoother transitions, controlled pacing, and a more cohesive interpretation of the piece.

Beyond the overarching rhythmic structure, the second scan should also allow you to identify (and definitely mark) any relevant deviations from the established rhythmic patterns. Maybe you spotted irregular groupings in a few particular measures or there is a significant change in the larger rhythmic structures. These details can subtly or drastically impact phrasing and momentum. Mark any sequences, motifs, or groupings that will help guide your sight-reading.

Form and Structure

The third and final horizontal scan reveals the blueprint of the music, allowing you to shape phrasing, dynamics, and pacing with intention. While more subtle than the previous scans, this step is crucial for identifying repetitions, sectional contrasts, and structural cues that will influence interpretation. The form and structure of a composition provides the road-map for musical flow, ensuring the performance feels natural rather than mechanical. This finalizes the Horizontal Framework Development, integrating all previous scans into a cohesive, structured understanding of the score before you play.

Every piece adheres to a structural logic. Identifying where sections begin and end, where themes return, and where contrasts occur is crucial for shaping interpretation. Without this awareness, transitions might feel abrupt, climaxes could lose their impact, and the overall narrative of the piece might become unclear. Recognizing these key structural points allows for a deliberate, controlled interpretation rather than reactive playing. The structure uncovered in this final scan now integrates with your knowledge of history and theory, transforming sight-reading a fluid, controlled, and intuitive process.

The final horizontal scan eliminates macro-uncertainties, setting the stage for a controlled sight-reading process. By this point, you've established a familiar framework, ensuring that the tempo, phrasing, and structural landmarks are already mapped out. With this blueprint in place, sight-reading becomes less about reacting and more about executing within a system you've already internalized.

Title & Context

Some might argue that this chapter should have started by focusing on the title. Unfortunately, that approach invites dangerous assumptions. If you were to see the word "Sonata" on the title, you might convince yourself you already know the framework and skip the scans entirely. However, this assumption will provide an incorrect framework since no real work was done. This ultimately results in poor sight-reading habits. The framework must come from the score itself, not from preconceived notions. Relying on the title first puts you in a blind spot you won't notice until it's too late.

Nevertheless, the title is fundamental and must be included as a part of the Horizontal Framework as it might validate the framework or reveal interpretative nuances that weren't a result of the scans. The character, mood, and intention of a piece might embedded in its title and will come into play when choosing a tempo to perform the piece. More than just a label, the title offers direct insight into the music's meaning. It serves as a gateway into the composer's vision, offering a glimpse of the energy, structure, or emotional depth that lies within the score.

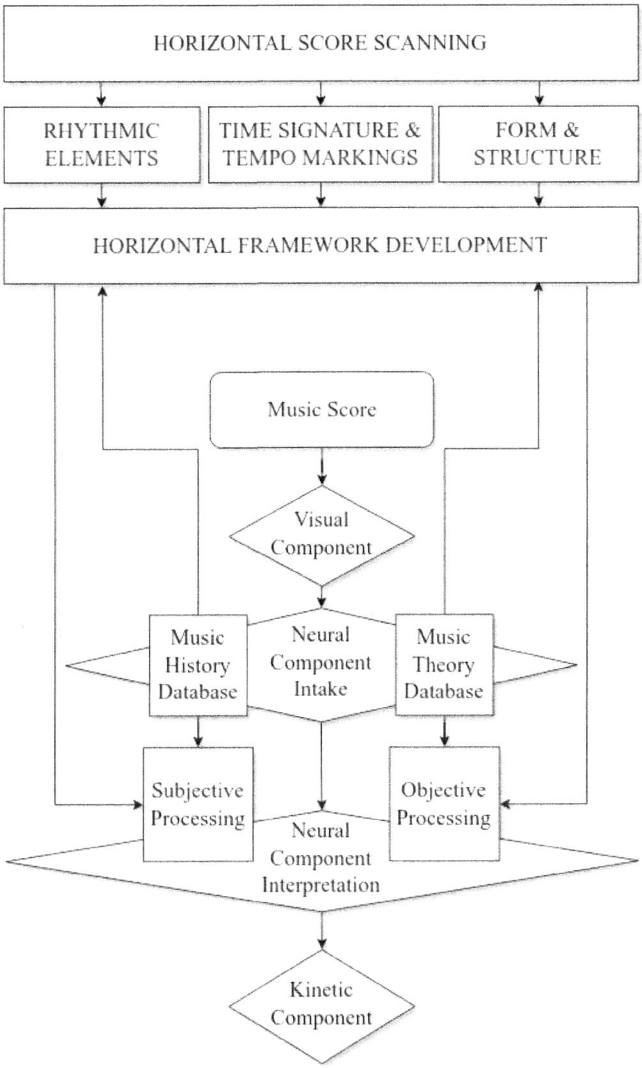

Reflections

Every time you jump into a piece without developing a Horizontal Framework, you set yourself up for confusion, hesitation, and failure from the very start. A strong Horizontal Framework provides a clear understanding of the two-dimensional geography of the musical score. You'll recognize landmarks, spot the fastest routes, anticipate shortcuts, and locate the structural signposts that support smooth sight-reading. With this preparation in place, you're ready for a more confident and fluid journey through the music. Challenges become easier to manage, and tempo becomes a tool you can use to your advantage.

Prompt: Using a pencil, take a new score within your technical grasp and execute the three levels of Horizontal Scan in the correct order. Avoid playing the piece. How long did the three scans take? Could you have done it faster? Were there any big reveals thanks to those scans? Did you begin forming a horizontal framework for this score? Did you discover a gap in your knowledge that needs attention? Could you have completed this process in an audition setting? If so, how might it have impacted your sight-reading execution before playing a single note?

Your Horizontal Framework is designed to support anticipation rather than perfection. It offers a clear roadmap for navigating time-based elements, helping you stay aligned with tempo, rhythm, and structure. Yet sight-reading also relies on a deeper layer of awareness. Vertical Score Scanning introduces that next level—uncovering harmonic textures, intervallic relationships, and note groupings. Combined, these approaches create a unified system for processing music as it unfolds in real time.

CHAPTER FIVE

The Vertical Perspective of Music

"90%! That's the bare minimum to be considered acceptable in the world of music. Actually! You could nail every note, but miss just one at the wrong time, and it's still a failure. So what is 50% in music? We probably shouldn't even ask! At this point, attempting to sight-read music without scanning the harmonies and melodies is like trying to run a marathon with one shoe... and its' untied. Don't be surprised if the tomatoes start flying."

Introduction

Vertical Score Scanning is the foundation of harmonic and melodic fluency in sight-reading. While horizontal scanning structures time and form, vertical scanning defines how sound unfolds in real time. Harmony, melody, and texture do not exist in isolation—they shape each other simultaneously. Without analyzing this interaction, sight-reading remains unpredictable and unstable.

Music unfolds in layers. Each vertical moment in a score carries harmonic significance—some notes establish the key, others introduce motion, and some bring resolution. Learning to identify these roles ahead of time reduces hesitation and supports more accurate execution. When key changes, dissonances, or harmonic shifts feel disorienting, it often points to a gap in vertical scanning. Strengthening this skill shifts the experience from reactive to intentional, giving you greater control over how the music is read and performed.

This is where Vertical Framework Development comes in. It is not a rigid set of rules but a guideline that prepares the field for proper execution. It defines parameters that help sight-reading function fluently in melody, harmony, and texture. Tonal centers provide stability, chord progressions shape the harmonic flow, and melodic lines determine phrasing and direction. By scanning vertically before playing, you establish the structural awareness needed to navigate the music with confidence.

A key strategy involves working backward. Starting from the resolution reveals how harmonic tensions are shaped, making it easier to understand the path leading to that point. Recognizing where the music settles enhances your sense of direction, helping you anticipate changes rather than react to them. This method draws attention to structural anchors—cadences, modulations, and harmonic pivots—that guide the flow of the piece. Instead of approaching a score without orientation, scanning from the resolution establishes a clearer harmonic framework before you begin to play. Vertical scanning plays a central role in connecting harmonic understanding with real-time performance, making sight-reading more stable and intentional.

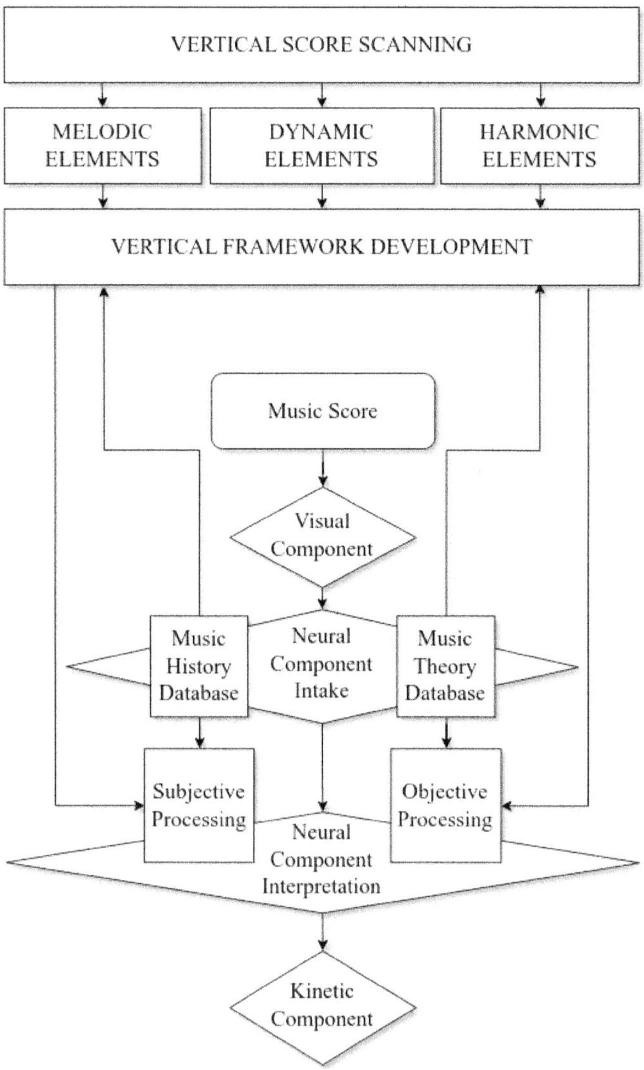
VERTICAL SCORE SCANNING
MELODIC ELEMENTS
DYNAMIC ELEMENTS
HARMONIC ELEMENTS
VERTICAL FRAMEWORK DEVELOPMENT
Music Score
Visual Component
Music History Database
Neural Component Intake
Music Theory Database
Subjective Processing
Objective Processing
Neural Component Interpretation
Kinetic Component

Keys and Alterations

The first step in vertical scanning is identifying the tonal foundation—everything else builds from there. Without a clear key, harmonic phrasing has no structure, and melodic analysis floats without reference. This scan establishes the tonal center by locating the key signature, as well as the first and last notes in the score. These anchor points clarify where the music begins, where it wants to go, and how it resolves. Starting here ensures that every harmonic layer to follow makes sense. It's a simple scan, but its impact on confidence and control is immediate and lasting.

While the key signature provides an initial framework, the true definition of the piece often lies in its ending. The final chord or note confirms, contradicts, or reshapes the expected tonality. A conclusive resolution reinforces the established key, while a deceptive cadence, modulation, or unexpected harmonic shift can reveal a dual tonal structure. A piece could also be divided into a minor and a major section allowing the interpreter to explore contrasting approaches. A Picardy third, on the other side can completely redefine the entire piece by simply shifting from minor to major at the very last second.

These details—modulations, tonal shifts, and deceptive cadences—are what give a piece its expressive depth. A quick but focused scan often reveals these interpretive cues early on. When these moments go unnoticed, transitions may feel unstable or awkward in performance. That's why this step requires clarity and concentration: just a few seconds spent analyzing key areas can illuminate the harmonic structure with surprising accuracy. Tonality isn't just academic—it's the binding force that holds musical meaning together. Recognizing it early transforms uncertainty into informed phrasing and prepares the mind for confident execution.

Chords and Chord Progressions

A second scan focused on chord progressions reveals the harmonic foundation of a piece. This layer of Vertical Framework Development is essential for understanding how harmonies evolve, resolve, and interact with melodic lines in real time. Without it, sight-reading becomes reactive rather than intentional, as the harmonic flow dictates phrasing, tension, and resolution.

Most chords will align with the key signature, which is expected. The goal of this scan is not to confirm what is obvious but to anticipate harmonic surprises. The most critical harmonic pillars to identify are the tonic and dominant chords, as they push the narrative forward. The tonic provides stability, while the dominant generates momentum, setting up inevitable resolutions. Recognizing where these occur allows for smoother phrasing and harmonic clarity.

The next priority is functional chords that introduce accidentals, signaling harmonic deviations. The Neapolitan chord, for example, is built on the lowered second scale degree and often prepares the dominant, creating a heightened sense of drama. Augmented sixth chords, which incorporate chromaticism to intensify resolution, serve a similar function. These chords disrupt conventional expectations, making them essential to identify before playing.

Finally, the scan must account for temporary modulations, often marked by key signature changes or a sequence of accidentals that establish a secondary key. These shifts temporarily reorient harmonic function, requiring realignment of tonic-dominant relationships. If unnoticed, interpretation of harmonic phrasing is at risk.

Of course, this scan should be fast but deliberate, pinpointing essential harmonic landmarks and marking the score where needed. Vertical Framework Development in this context ensures that each harmonic shift is anticipated in advance, providing a clear harmonic trajectory. When these elements are overlooked, uncertainty increases. But when the framework is in place, sight-reading aligns with the natural flow of the music, allowing for clarity, precision, and expressive depth.

Melodic Elements

The third and final scan focuses on melody, the element that bridges both horizontal and vertical dimensions of music. This is where all prior scans—harmonic, rhythmic, and structural—converge into a complete and cohesive interpretation. Melodies define a composition's identity, carrying its expressive weight and shaping its narrative arc. While harmony and rhythm provide the framework, melody is what ultimately leaves a lasting impression on both the performer and the audience.

This scan comes last because melodic motion relies on the elements previously established. When harmonic awareness is missing, melodies lack a stable foundation. If structural clarity is absent, their direction becomes harder to interpret. By this point, Vertical Framework Development has already defined tonal stability, harmonic function, and structural divisions, allowing the melody to take its rightful place as the central expressive force.

A melody is not just a series of notes—it is the articulation of a musical thought. It moves through harmonic landscapes, interacts with rhythm, and defines phrasing. Identifying the melodic contour is crucial, as it dictates how tension and resolution unfold in real time. The interplay between melody and harmony must be fully understood, especially when internal modulations or harmonic deviations influence phrasing. The goal of this scan is to isolate, internalize, and elevate the melodic material within the broader framework.

To integrate this scan effectively, engage actively with the melody. Sing it internally, feel its phrasing, and observe its motion within the harmonic structure. Treat the composition as a choral arrangement rather than focusing solely on the top voice—melodies exist throughout the texture, shaping the piece's overall motion. Skipping this final step leaves sight-reading disjointed, driven by reaction instead of control. When this layer is in place, all elements of the music align, allowing phrasing, articulation, and structure to flow with precision.

Reflections

Jumping into a piece before applying Vertical Framework Development is like trying to interpret a conversation in an unfamiliar language. You might catch a few words, but the meaning remains unclear. A strong Vertical Framework provides the harmonic and melodic structure that stabilizes the reading process. It defines tonal centers, highlights harmonic motion, and clarifies the melodic pathways embedded within the score. Lacking this foundation turns each measure into an isolated event, disconnected from the overall narrative.

As the scanning process becomes habitual, music reveals itself as a connected architecture rather than a string of isolated notes. Harmonic shifts and modulations begin to stand out as navigational markers rather than unexpected turns. Melodic development takes on direction, shaped by the underlying tonal framework already in mind. What once felt like a test of survival becomes something more deliberate—a real-time conversation with the composer, guided by structure, logic, and expressive intent.

Skipping this step means misreading tonal centers, missing key modulations, and failing to recognize harmonic tensions before they unfold. The result? An interpretation that lacks direction, clarity, and expressive depth. By making Vertical Framework Development a habitual part of score preparation, you ensure that every piece has structural integrity before playing a single note.

Prompt: Take a score you have never played before and execute the three levels of Vertical Scan in order—key and tonal structure, harmonic progression, and melodic phrasing. Avoid playing the piece. How long did it take? Did you identify any modulations, harmonic pivots, or unexpected shifts? Could you have done it faster? Would this scan have prevented hesitation in a sight-reading setting? How would applying this process before an audition impact your confidence?

Vertical scanning focuses less on playing flawlessly and more on reading with intention, anticipating movement, and reducing uncertainty. When this skill is underdeveloped, sight-reading tends to feel unpredictable. When it's active, fluency improves, control increases, and real-time interpretation becomes far more attainable.

CHAPTER SIX

Finding the Right Tempo for a Balanced Execution

"Tempo is both an anchor and an illusion. The mind perceives it, the body executes it, and the listener experiences it—all differently. A pulse is steady, yet time stretches and contracts in the hands of a performer. Too rigid, and it feels lifeless. Too loose, and it loses clarity. Musicians obsess over beats per minute, yet tempo isn't a number—it's momentum, weight, and breath. It's not just how fast or slow. It's how time feels."

Introduction

Tempo bridges the neural (brain) and kinetic (body) aspects of music-making, ensuring they work in harmony for peak performance. Beyond its technical role, tempo shapes the aesthetic and emotional character of music, connecting execution with interpretation. It is more than measurement—it is an expressive force. Composers embed breath and motion into their music, shaping its natural flow. Tempo that is too rigid feels lifeless, while neglecting precision weakens clarity. Your goal is to find a tempo that highlights your skill while preserving the music's emotional depth.

In sight-reading, tempo determines whether you stay in control or lose momentum. Your ability may allow you to play faster than indicated, but the right tempo conveys the essence of the piece. The challenge is to find a tempo that fits your ability while honoring the music's expressive demands.

Success is ultimately defined by the audience's experience. A performance that balances technical control and emotional resonance leaves a lasting impression. By integrating insights from Chapter 2 (History and Theory), Chapter 3 (Technical Mastery), and the analytical tools from Chapters 4 & 5, tempo selection becomes more than a technical task—it becomes a tool for storytelling, ensuring a balance between composer intent and personal interpretation.

Key Considerations for Tempo Selection

Selecting the right tempo requires balancing technical execution, clarity, and musical emotion, all informed by the horizontal and vertical scanning frameworks. Without understanding rhythmic structure, harmonic flow, and form, tempo selection becomes arbitrary. To ensure that tempo enhances rather than hinders performance, ask yourself:

Does this speed allow phrasing and expression to emerge naturally?

Am I sacrificing musical intent for technical security?

Does this tempo align with historical and stylistic expectations?

By reflecting on these factors, you avoid mechanical rigidity and ensure that tempo serves the artistic vision of the music—even when sight-reading at first glance. These questions serve as a practical guide whether you are preparing a new piece, sight-reading, or adjusting tempo in real time during performance.

Self-Awareness

The best tempo strikes a balance—precise enough for control, free enough for expression. In sight-reading, this balance is fragile since perception of time shifts under pressure. If a passage feels technically limiting, resist the urge to slow down excessively; instead, focus on efficiency and phrasing. Conversely, don't chase speed at the cost of clarity. The key is blending accuracy with passion, allowing confidence without compromise. Though tempo is measurable, subjective perception distorts it. Mood, adrenaline, and stage dynamics can make time feel elastic—a relaxed performer may rush, while tension can slow a passage. Mastering these shifts ensures stability in performance.

Tempo should breathe with the music, shaped by horizontal elements like phrase lengths and transitions, and vertical elements like harmonic density and modulations. Accuracy honors the score's structure, while passion connects you to the audience through emotional expression. Sacrificing either diminishes performance quality. Rigid adherence to tempo markings may lead to lifeless delivery, while excessive expression risks losing clarity.

Choosing the right tempo starts with preparation. Conduct horizontal and vertical scans to assess phrasing, harmony, and technical challenges. This ensures tempo aligns with both musical integrity and your ability. For technically demanding pieces, a slightly slower tempo can maintain precision while allowing the music's emotional essence to unfold. Horizontal scanning determines overarching pacing, while vertical scanning reveals harmonic and melodic details that shape phrasing.

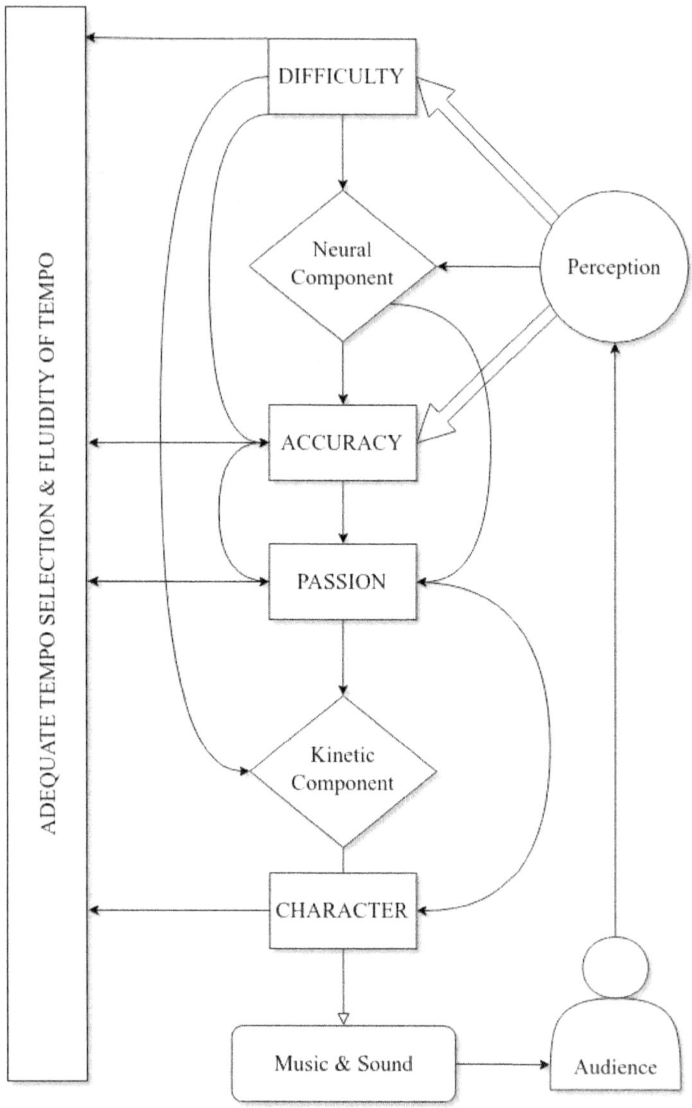

Difficulty

Once you have conducted the horizontal and vertical scans outlined in previous chapters, you will have a clear understanding of the difficulty level of a piece. This insight allows you to approach the music with a positive mindset by categorizing it into three zones:

Within the Comfort Zone: The Comfort Zone is not about ease—it is about fluency. A piece in this category is one where accuracy is no longer the primary challenge. You can execute the notes, rhythms, and dynamics reliably at tempo. There is no fight, no hesitation, no breakdown of coordination. Your hands, your ear, and your reading reflexes work together without struggle. Because the mechanics are secure, your mind is no longer consumed by survival. You are free to explore deeper layers—shaping tone, refining articulation, stretching interpretation. This is where technical control transforms into musical freedom.

On the Edge of the Comfort Zone: This is where fluency begins to stretch—where your control is tested, but not broken. The piece is playable, yet it demands more from you. Perhaps the tempo feels just beyond your instinctive reach, or certain passages require heightened focus to maintain precision. Here, you must trust the process. Doubt slows you down; hesitation creates mistakes. Instead of fearing the challenge, lean into it. Adjust the tempo if needed, but never at the cost of the music's integrity. This is where your limits expand—not through caution, but through conviction. There is no room for distractions.

Outside the Comfort Zone: Here, the music moves faster than your reflexes, the patterns feel unpredictable, and the technical demands outweigh your immediate capacity. Instinct tells you to chase the tempo, to force speed where there is no stability. Resist that impulse. Slowing down is not retreat—it is the only way to take control. Stretch time until every note becomes clear, every movement intentional. Give your brain the space to process before your hands react. Precision first, momentum second. If the music feels too fast, it means you haven't yet made it yours. Own the tempo now, and mastery will follow.

Those classifications tie directly into Chapter 3's principles of technical mastery—recognizing where your current skills stand and how to challenge them strategically, especially when sight-reading requires split-second tempo decisions. Mastery involves gradually expanding your comfort zone with intention. Choosing the right tempo helps you balance technical accuracy with expressive depth, turning moments of difficulty into opportunities for focused development.

Prompt: Select a new piece of music that falls within your technical grasp. Apply both the horizontal and vertical scans before playing. Execute the piece and then reflect on how the process unfolded. Consider how staying within your technical grasp influenced your confidence and control. Reflect on what worked well and identify areas for improvement. How could this process and feeling be adapted to tackle more challenging pieces effectively? How did staying within your grasp affect your confidence and performance? What adjustments would help translate this sense of control and success to more challenging pieces?

Experience expands your comfort zone by strengthening decision-making gradually, just as Chapter 3 emphasized technical mastery as a long-term process. Over time, you build a mental and emotional reservoir that supports informed decision-making. Success depends more on your approach than on the difficulty itself. Mastering a piece is not about avoiding challenges but about managing them intelligently, ensuring control even when stepping beyond your limits.

Accuracy

Accuracy is the foundation of musical performance—the bridge between honoring the score and making it your own. It is not about perfection, but about clarity, fidelity, and control. True accuracy is intentional, not mechanical. In sight-reading, this means processing information quickly while maintaining clarity—balancing execution and expression in real time.

Yet, accuracy does not exist on the page—it is shaped by the brain and executed by the body. The neural system perceives, recognizes, and makes decisions, while the kinetic system converts those decisions into movement. Mastery comes when these processes work seamlessly together.

Accuracy relies on three key elements: technical command, score awareness, and controlled flexibility. Technical mastery ensures that mechanics do not interfere with interpretation. Score understanding allows musicians to anticipate structure, phrasing, and potential challenges. Control and flexibility prevent accuracy from becoming rigid, ensuring that precision serves musicality rather than restricting it.

The goal is not just to play the right notes, but to shape them with confidence and purpose. Accuracy is not about eliminating mistakes—it is about maintaining clarity, control, and expression, even in the face of the unexpected.

Prompt: Choose a piece that lies on the edge of your technical grasp. Slow the tempo significantly—to the point where mistakes are nearly impossible. Execute the piece at this reduced speed, focusing entirely on accuracy and clarity. Reflect on how the slower tempo impacted your connection with the music and your control over the score. What adjustments would be necessary to maintain this level of precision at a higher tempo? How does this process shape your approach to mastering more challenging pieces?

This is where neural-to-kinetic synchronization becomes essential. As explored in Chapter 3, your brain processes musical data faster than your hands can execute it. The goal of accuracy training is not just to execute the correct notes but to create a seamless feedback loop between perception, decision-making, and execution. And as we have seen in chapter 2, this is why MIDI playback, though technically flawless, lacks artistry. Mechanical perfection does not equate to musical mastery. A great performer does not just hit the right notes—they shape them. Your goal is to balance precision with expression, using technique to serve musical storytelling rather than sounding rigid or artificial.

Passion

Passion elevates performance from accurate to unforgettable. Music is not simply executed—it's lived and felt. It creates a bridge between performer and audience, shaped as much by emotion as by intention. Passion doesn't arise out of nowhere; it's cultivated through knowledge, historical understanding, and the performer's mental and emotional state.

A deep understanding of theory, historical context, and the composer's intent refines emotion rather than restricting it. The same passage may feel triumphant to one musician and melancholic to another. A piece that once felt neutral can become devastating, electrifying, or playful depending on your emotional state.

On stage, passion is magnified—some musicians tremble before a solo, only to have that energy explode into power. Others enter a flow state where emotions pour effortlessly into the music. Recognizing how mental and physical states impact passion allows you to harness it rather than be consumed by it.

Passion without clarity can easily turn into chaos. Every phrase should convey a clear idea, unfolding with purpose rather than pressure. Tempo breathes within the music, offering space for expression while maintaining stability. A well-placed rubato can deepen emotion, while a sudden surge in tempo may inject urgency. Interpretation involves more than feeling—it requires thoughtful shaping and control. Passion drives the performance, but structure gives it direction. When these elements work in harmony, music doesn't simply move—it communicates.

Passion and technique are deeply intertwined—passion gives technique its voice. A delicate rubato can stir deep emotion, a sudden tempo shift can spark excitement, and a well-timed pause can captivate an audience. When expressive intent is supported by precision, execution evolves into a performance filled with emotional depth and resonance.

Prompt: Select a section of a piece you already know. Experiment with tempo fluctuations to heighten emotions—slow it down dramatically, pause unexpectedly, or push the tempo forward with urgency. How do these shifts change the emotional impact? Could you make a passage feel more desperate, more hopeful, or more volatile just by altering the pulse? How would your current emotional state affect this process?

Character

Every piece of music tells a story, and tempo is the key to bringing it to life. This is why you worked through difficulty, refined accuracy, and ignited passion—because character is where they all converge. It's not just about playing the notes; it's about shaping the narrative within them.

Character is understanding the music's voice, channeling its emotions, and delivering them with conviction—even in sight-reading, where instinct must replace preparation. This is where technique disappears and storytelling begins. A phrase played too rigidly feels lifeless; a phrase without accuracy loses clarity. But when tempo, control, and expression align, the piece breathes.

Music is a conversation between harmony and melody, between intention and execution. The composer provides the foundation, but the performer gives it shape. Harmonies set the stage, phrasing guides momentum, and articulation defines the nuances of speech within the music. The right tempo allows these elements to unfold with clarity.

A piece is not just a sequence of notes—it is a journey shaped by interpretation, creativity, and personal insight. When character is fully realized, the audience doesn't just hear the music—they experience its meaning. And when that meaning is clear, every note resonates with purpose.

This is why tempo matters. It was never just about playing in time—it was about playing with meaning. You can master technique, execute with accuracy, and perform with passion, but without character, the music remains incomplete. When tempo is chosen with intention, everything aligns—difficulty becomes fluency, accuracy becomes clarity, passion becomes connection. The music transcends notes and becomes an experience.

Prompt: Select a piece within your technical grasp. Conduct thorough horizontal and vertical scans, identifying key voices, harmonic tension, and expressive markings. Play the piece with full awareness of these elements. How does emphasizing different voices reshape the narrative? How do tempo shifts alter emotional impact? How can this apply to more advanced pieces?

Reflections

As we have seen in the concepts outlined in this section, choosing the correct tempo is more than just playing at the right speed—it's about shaping time itself. When precision meets character, music stops being a mechanical exercise and becomes a living, breathing art form. The tempo you choose is not just a reflection of the score—it's a reflection of you: your skill, your interpretation, and your ability to channel expression through structure.

Choosing the right tempo requires balancing difficulty, accuracy, passion, and character. Sight-reading cannot happen without about technical control, artistic vision, and connection to the music, even when interpreting at first glance. Play too rigidly, and you risk lifeless precision; ignore control, and passion becomes chaos. The true balance lies where discipline and emotion meet—where structure supports expression rather than restricting it.

Tempo selection unites every skill you have developed—from theory and technical mastery (Chapters 2 & 3) to phrasing and harmonic awareness (Chapters 4 & 5). But who you are playing for defines how you shape time.

Your audience is not limited to a concert hall. At times, you are your own listener, evaluating fluency as you refine your skills. In an audition, a juror measures your ability to interpret and execute under pressure. In an ensemble, your colleagues depend on your rhythmic awareness to maintain cohesion. Even in a casual setting, a listener—peer, teacher, or friend—experiences the decisions you make in real time. The tempo you choose defines the way your music is heard, felt, and understood, and this decision should always be rooted in insights gained from horizontal and vertical scanning.

Therefore, sight-reading is more than a technical skill—it is the foundation of musical fluency. You are no longer simply decoding notes; you are translating sound into meaning. The ability to take a score and give it shape, energy, and breath is what separates a player from an artist.

You have built a strong foundation, but execution alone is not enough. A musician's greatest challenge is not just technical—it's mental. How do you handle the unexpected? What happens when nerves distort your sense of time? How do you recover from a shaky start or regain control when the adrenaline surges? Mastering tempo is not just about controlling the music—it's about controlling yourself. The next section will take you beyond execution and into the world of mindset, self-perception, and resilience. In the end, time does not control you. You control time. And if you do it right, no one will hear the tempo—only the music as you have adequately interpreted it.

SECTION THREE

Overcoming the Past, Excelling in the Present, and Defining the Future

Introduction

You have spent the first two sections of this book mastering the mechanics of sight-reading: understanding its structure, refining execution, and developing habits that align with your strengths. Now, we shift to an even more powerful arena. What happens when everything technical is in place, yet performance remains inconsistent? Why do some musicians thrive under pressure while others hesitate? What separates those who flow effortlessly through sight-reading from those who stumble at the first mistake?

The answer lies beyond the notes—not in technique alone, but in the mind behind the music. How you process the past, engage with the present, and project into the future shapes not just your performance, but your ability to sight-read fluently, under pressure, and without hesitation. Section III explores the unseen yet profoundly influential factors that determine whether you can navigate unfamiliar music smoothly—or whether hesitation, tension, and doubt will hold you back.

Here, we step outside the direct mechanics of sight-reading and examine what is happening in the background—your perceptions, habits, and internal dialogue. These elements do not exist on the score, yet they define how well you play it. Mastering them is the key to performing at your highest level, not only in sight-reading but in every musical challenge you face.

Shifting the Mindset for Effortless Reading

The work you have done so far has prepared you to read music fluently, efficiently, and with greater confidence. Section I broke down the foundations—how visual input, neural processing, kinetic execution, and auditory feedback work in constant motion. Section II trained your approach—how to scan a score, make quick decisions, and execute with precision.

Preparation alone is not enough. Your habits, emotions, and mindset determine whether that training holds up when it matters most. What happens inside your mind in the seconds after a mistake? How well can you stay present under pressure? Can you step into an unfamiliar piece with a clear sense of readiness, or does doubt cloud your judgment?

This section is about developing the inner mastery needed to elevate everything else you have learned so far. It is about freeing your mind from hesitation, sharpening your presence, and actively shaping your performance before it even happens.

Refining the Mind

This final section moves through three critical dimensions—the past, present, and future—each addressed in a dedicated chapter. These are mental skills, just as vital as technique itself. These chapters will equip you with the tools to break free from hesitation, sharpen your focus, and make sight-reading—and your entire musical experience—fluid and fearless. Mastery of sight-reading is not just about reading new music; it's about training your mind to remain fluid, adaptable, and unshaken in any musical challenge.

The mental discipline you develop here will not only refine your sight-reading—it will elevate your phrasing, enhance your ability to respond to ensemble dynamics, and solidify your presence in every performance, whether it is a memorized piece or a sight-reading session.

Past: A mistake is a single event, yet for many musicians, it snowballs into doubt, hesitation, or self-sabotage. Why? Because the mind clings to it. Instead of flowing forward, many musicians become trapped in a loop of self-criticism and overcorrection—turning a single wrong note into a performance-derailing event.

Present: Musicians often believe that practice alone will make them better performers, yet distraction, tension, and scattered focus still undermine their execution. Peak sight-reading demands absolute presence—a mental state free from external noise, stress, and hesitation. By improving your daily life—sleep, nutrition, and mental conditioning—you will unlock the clarity and stability necessary to execute at your highest level every time you perform.

Future: Visualization is not about wishful thinking—it is about preconditioning your nervous system to handle unpredictability with confidence. This chapter teaches you how to step into an unfamiliar score already mentally prepared, ensuring that when the moment comes, you are not hesitating, guessing, or hoping—you are simply executing what you have already trained your mind to do.

The Cost of Ignoring Mental Mastery

Ignore these tools, and the same cycle returns: flow breaks, reactions slow, and your sense of control collapses—not from lack of practice, but from an untrained mind. Sight-reading remains fragile, not from lack of skill, but from untrained focus, unresolved hesitation, and mental habits left unchecked.

You will remain trapped in a cycle of inconsistency. Despite all your preparation, the same problems will resurface: hesitation, self-doubt, and the inability to recover from mistakes. Progress will plateau—not because of your technique, but because your mindset was never trained to support it. You may learn new pieces, refine your skills, and expand your repertoire, but if hesitation still governs your sight-reading, it will infect everything you play. Fluency is not just a skill—it's a state of mind. Even in memorized music, unresolved tension and doubt will creep in, undermining your freedom and expression. Mental strength lets you recover. Focus gives you resilience. Confidence is not a result—it's a habit. Without these principles, every breakthrough becomes temporary, every success fragile. Growth stalls. Performance never feels effortless.

If you fail to let go of mistakes, your playing will always carry the weight of past errors. One wrong note can send you spiraling, derailing your focus and breaking your fluency. Instead of moving forward, you become stuck—trapped in a loop of self-correction and frustration, unable to execute with clarity and control.

If you fail to cultivate focus, distractions will dictate your performance. Your attention will drift at the worst moments, tension will creep into your body, and your execution will suffer. You will find yourself mentally scattered—overwhelmed by nerves, thrown off by external noise, or losing control when your thoughts race ahead instead of staying with the music.

If you fail to train your mind for the future, every musical moment will feel like a gamble. You'll step onto the stage uncertain, hoping for a good outcome instead of ensuring one. Without visualization, your nervous system won't be prepared to handle pressure, and the unpredictability of live situations will take over. You don't rise to the occasion—you fall to the level of your preparation. When the mind isn't conditioned, every mistake, distraction, and unknown becomes an obstacle instead of something you can navigate.

Reflections

This final section transforms you into the kind of musician who doesn't just prepare—but arrives ready. Ready to adapt, to recover, to lead. Sight-reading is no longer a technical hurdle—it becomes a mental art form, shaped by discipline, sharpened by pressure, and anchored in presence. When mental discipline is lacking, even the most polished technique can collapse under pressure. The goal now is to remove that uncertainty and reinforce everything you've built—so that when the moment arrives, you are not just capable, but unshakable.

The strategies here are not passive ideas to consider but principles to embody. They require deliberate action, reflection, and refinement until they become second nature. You cannot hope to feel grounded—you must train that stability. You cannot wait for focus—you must cultivate it. Mastery is not given; it is forged through disciplined habits and a relentless commitment to growth.

Every moment spent dwelling on past mistakes is a moment stolen from the present. Every distraction entertained in practice is a seed of inconsistency that will grow when it matters most. Every doubt left unchecked takes root and resurfaces under pressure. If your mind becomes a battleground of hesitation and self-criticism, every note will be at its mercy. But when you train the mind like an instrument, the stage becomes a space of clarity—not a battlefield of doubt. With clarity, control, and intent, your musical expression is no longer a test of endurance—it becomes a space for execution, interpretation, and freedom.

Sight-reading is not just about reading—it is about trust: trust in your mind, your reflexes, and your ability to navigate the unknown. And that trust extends beyond sight-reading—it fuels clarity, precision, and expressive freedom in every note you play. The stronger that trust becomes, the more effortless all of your music will feel.

CHAPTER SEVEN

BREAKING THE MISTAKE LOOP: REWIRING FOR PROGRESS

"WHAT A MESS! HUMANITY stumbles, falls, wrecks itself. Yet here we are, still pushing forward. The past is a foundation, not a prison, and self-sabotage is dead weight. Praise the good notes. Leave the errors behind. Music, history, and everything else will move forward... with or without you on board."

Introduction

The past exists only in memory, yet it constantly tries to shape the present. Mistakes, once made, are gone—they no longer exist in reality, only in recollection. But the mind clings to them, replaying errors, assigning them weight, and allowing them to influence what happens next. In sight-reading, this attachment is the ultimate disruption.

A mistake is simply a deviation from expectation—a note that didn't match intent. But the experience of a mistake is subjective. One musician might notice an incorrect note and move on, while another spirals into frustration. The difference is not the mistake itself but how the mind processes it. If the brain assigns it significance, hesitation follows. If the musician fixates, fluency is broken. Sight-reading demands forward motion, yet the past—through memory, judgment, and emotional conditioning—pulls attention backward.

Letting go of mistakes is not about pretending they don't happen. It's about refusing to let them define what comes next. This chapter dissects why mistakes take hold, why the past fights to dictate the present, and how to dismantle the mental traps that turn errors into anchors. Sight-reading is not about perfection; it is about adaptability. To master it, the musician must learn to process mistakes—not as failures, but as fleeting moments already behind them.

Understanding the trap

Mistakes happen. They are inevitable in sight-reading—a natural result of navigating unfamiliar terrain in real time. Yet not all musicians react the same way. Some acknowledge an error and move on. Others let a single wrong note drag them backward, anchoring them in a spiral of self-doubt, overcorrection, and frustration. This is the trap.

The neural component of music processing is both a guide and a judge. It interprets notes, commands the body, evaluates execution. But when a mistake occurs, it can turn against the musician, amplifying the undesired instance far beyond its actual significance. Instead of moving forward, the brain fixates, replaying the failure, recalling similar past mistakes, and flooding the mind with criticism. The result? The present moment is lost.

Sight-reading offers no luxury of stopping, fixing, or reliving. Unlike prepared performance, where muscle memory can compensate, sight-reading demands forward momentum. Hesitation is destruction. Clinging to a misstep for even a moment can derail the entire process. Pride and fear are the core triggers of the trap.

Pride: Inadequate self-perception misleads the musician into believing that skill is defined by flawlessness. Pride becomes a false armor of self-worth. When something goes wrong, pride reframes it as a personal failure rather than a passing event. The mind resists the disruption, triggering self-justification, frustration, or anger—anything to protect the illusion of perfection. This tension tightens the body, fractures concentration, and turns a single lapse into many. Instead of processing the moment and moving forward, pride forces fixation, making sight-reading a battle not against the music, but against the self.

Fear: The mind misinterprets mistakes as threats, trapping the musician in hesitation. Fear is the weight of past failures, dragging sight-reading into a battle with memory instead of music. Each wrong note is not just an error—it is a trigger, reviving old embarrassments, criticism, and self-doubt. The brain resists the present, replaying past failures and anticipating new ones. This paralysis disrupts neural flow, tightening the body and clouding judgment. Instead of adapting and moving forward, fear locks the musician in a loop where hesitation breeds more mistakes, making sight-reading not an act of fluency, but of avoidance.

Wired from Childhood

A musician's journey begins long before picking up an instrument. The brain forms associations with success and failure, praise and criticism, long before the first note is played. By the time a musician sits down to sight-read, mistakes are not just errors—they are filtered through a lifetime of conditioning. The human brain is wired for survival. Early humans depended on social cohesion, where failure could mean rejection or exile. That instinct remains. A wrong note, though harmless, can still trigger the same response—racing heart, tension, short breath. The body reacts as if mistakes are threats, disrupting focus and flow.

Sight-reading demands forward motion, yet mistakes pull the musician into the past, replaying failures and anticipating more. The real trap lies not in the mistake itself but how the brain clings to it, dragging past failures into the present. Fortunately, just as fear can be learned, it can also be unlearned. When mistakes are viewed as neutral events rather than personal failures, their impact begins to fade. With consistent awareness, exposure, and mental retraining, musicians can move toward a mindset where errors inform growth rather than hinder performance.

Childhood: Even when a sight-reading mistake is isolated, our relationship to that mistake awakens patterns wired long ago. A child's earliest encounters with failure—whether met with patience or punishment—shape how those situations feel. If mistakes once led to shame or disappointment, the brain learned to associate them with fear, tension, and self-doubt. Without early encouragement to see failure as growth, musicians internalize an unforgiving critic that revives every past mistake. In sight-reading, a single wrong note is never just a wrong note—it carries the weight of past corrections, past judgment, past hesitation, dragging the mind backward instead of forward.

Trauma: Deep-seated emotional wounds reshape how setbacks are perceived. When failure was met with public criticism or humiliation, those moments stopped being neutral—they became triggers. The brain is now conditioned to avoid pain by responding with self-attacks. A sight-reading slip is no longer just an isolated event; it revives the weight of past failures, the sting of judgment, the fear of exposure. Each disruption reinforces the belief that imperfections are not momentary lapses but evidence of inadequacy. Sight-reading becomes a battlefield where challenges are not just obstacles but threats, dragging the musician backward into a cycle of doubt and hesitation.

Relationships: In this trigger minefield, negative relationships could act as multipliers for the sensitivity of the triggers. Perfectionist mentors, critical peers, and judgmental spaces reinforce the fear, amplifying hesitation, keeping the musician trapped in a mindset where mistakes aren't just errors—they are life-threatening dangers.

The Brain & Memory

The neural component determines whether an observation gets marked as a mistake. Some errors pass unnoticed, while others linger—fueling hesitation and self-doubt. This process follows patterns rooted in experience. The brain doesn't merely register mistakes; it often fixates on them, linking them to past experiences, emotional triggers, or the immediate fear of judgment. What could be a fleeting moment of disruption instead becomes a reinforced signal, interrupting focus and destabilizing the sight-reading process.

This judgment is purely subconscious. Biological mechanisms regulate focus, memory, and emotional responses. When an error is flagged as significant, the body reacts before logic can intervene—tension rises, breathing shifts, and the mind spirals into correction mode. These automatic responses stem from the same neural systems that govern survival instincts, learning, and emotional regulation. To break free from fixation, we must understand how these systems shape our perception of mistakes.

The Frontal Lobe: The frontal lobe governs decision-making, pattern recognition, and problem-solving, acting as sight-reading's command center. It directs focus, plans movements, and adjusts execution. It determines whether to stay the course or make adjustments. When efficient, it overrides emotional reactions instantly. But overactivity leads to excessive self-monitoring, hesitation, and disrupted flow.

HINT: Training the frontal lobe requires repeated exposure to mistakes—forcing it to process errors as neutral events. The more it adapts, the less likely it is to trap the musician in a loop of overcorrection and lost momentum.

The Hippocampus: The hippocampus is the brain's memory center, storing and reinforcing sight-reading patterns. When a misstep is repeated, it strengthens neural pathways, increasing the likelihood of recurrence. This is why inefficient habits become ingrained unless deliberately overwritten. While it encodes technical patterns, it also works alongside the amygdala to attach emotional weight to challenging moments. Slips made under pressure receive priority storage, making them harder to forget.

HINT: The hippocampus is adaptable. Low-pressure, deliberate exposure to mistakes allows memory to be re-consolidated under neutral conditions, weakening their emotional grip. Practicing errors without judgment rewires recall, reshaping sight-reading for precision instead of fear.

The Amygdala: The amygdala assigns emotional weight to disruptions, deciding whether an event is neutral or a threat. In high-pressure situations—especially for musicians conditioned to fear imperfection—it triggers an immediate stress response, tightening focus on the disruption instead of the music. Heart rate spikes, muscles tense, and hesitation takes over. When this cycle repeats, these lapses are no longer isolated—they become anticipated, feeding preemptive anxiety.

HINT: The amygdala responds to perceived danger. Training under manageable stress incrementally, rather than avoiding it, desensitizes its reaction, allowing mistakes to happen without triggering panic.

Diffusing the Trap

Setbacks are inevitable, but their impact depends on how the mind reacts. Some musicians let disruptions pass, while others fixate—spiraling into self-doubt and hesitation. This fixation is the trap. Now, the focus shifts to breaking that cycle. Diffusing the trap is not about pretending issues don't happen, but about stripping them of their power—interrupting the chain reaction that turns a brief lapse into a full derailment.

To diffuse the trap, the musician must recalibrate their reaction, learning to process mistakes neutrally instead of emotionally. This shift is not about excusing errors but preventing them from derailing performance. By retraining emotional responses, and developing a forward-focused mindset, musicians can escape the cycle of fixation and hesitation.

Nevertheless, even with preemptive strategies to reduce their impact, mistakes will always trigger a reaction. The following three mechanisms are not just preventative—they must be deployed in real time during sight-reading. They allow you to seize control, rewire their impact, and shut them down before they hijack the performance.

Mindset: A mindset built for adaptability, not perfection, is essential for sight-reading. Focus ensures that errors do not pull attention backwards, by keeping a present state of mind. Mistake attempt to pull the mind backward. A trained mind interrupts this pull by anchoring itself in the present.

HINT: Recall the feeling of being fully present—the moment when time dissolves. What anchors you there? What subtle action can you trigger during sight-reading to instantly snap back into that state?

Resilience: Challenges will arise, but how you carry them defines your playing. Resilience means accepting unexpected moments without letting them shake your poise—the ability to stay composed and engaged rather than retreating into a defensive stance.

HINT: Identify moments in life where you either react with frustration or respond with confidence. What internal stance helps you face mistakes with control instead of defense? How can you train yourself to bring that same response into your sight-reading?

Judgment: Lapses need an overseer—they must be contained before they escalate. Judgment is the ability to apply discipline with precision, ensuring that momentary disruptions don't spiral into breakdown. Without a firm, objective stance, hesitation creeps in, breaking fluency. Sight-reading demands authority over these moments, allowing them to pass cleanly without derailing the momentum.

HINT: Judge the mistake ("That sucked") instead of yourself ("I suck"). Shift the error away from you, leaving it in a past tense. Treat mistakes like trash: Clean them up instantly so they never pile up in front of your sight-reading

Prompt: Now that you've explored Mindset, Resilience, and Judgment, how do they interact for you in sight-reading? Which mechanism comes naturally, and which one needs the most work? Can you identify past sight-reading sessions where fixation, hesitation, or emotional response took over? How could you have applied these tools in those moments? What adjustments can you make to train them as a real-time response rather than just concepts?

Reflections

Every mistake presents a choice. A wrong note disappears the moment it sounds. No amount of frustration or overcorrection can undo it. The real issue lies in how long you hold onto it. How much of your playing is shaped by errors that have already passed? The past often slips in quietly, creating the illusion that one misstep defines everything that follows. But mistakes only gain momentum when we give them power—your response determines whether they fade away or take over.

You've now learned how to break this cycle—to meet mistakes without hesitation, to acknowledge them without attachment, to move forward without fear. Mindset, resilience, and judgment are not just tools; they are your defense against the weight of past errors. Each time you apply them, you reinforce the skill of letting go, training yourself to process mistakes without letting them take hold.

The question is no longer "How do I avoid mistakes?" but "How do I prevent them from shaping what happens next?" Growth is not the absence of errors—it's the ability to stay composed in their presence, unshaken. You now can say that the past has no authority here. The next note does not wait for you to correct the last one. It only moves forward. It would be wise and adequate for you to also move on.

CHAPTER EIGHT

Mind & Body Synergy for Peak Performance

"You've let it slide long enough. Deep down, you know your habits have stifled your spark, disrupted your coordination, and making sight-reading harder than it should. It's not the notes—it's you... It was you all along."

Introduction

Balance forms the foundation of effective sight-reading. It supports steady hands, smooth eye movement, and clear mental processing. When that balance is disrupted, performance can begin to unravel, triggering a chain reaction of small breakdowns. Often, the issue doesn't come from the music itself, but from internal friction—tension, misalignment, or mental overload—that interferes with the flow of execution.

That friction has a source. It often stems from unaddressed habits, physical tension, or mental distractions. Fatigue, scattered focus, or slowed reaction time can quietly interfere with performance—even if these disruptions aren't immediately obvious. When sight-reading, their effects tend to surface. Achieving balance doesn't rely on vague feelings of being "relaxed" or "focused," but on identifying what's interfering and integrating what's missing. The goal is a body that moves with ease, a mind that stays grounded, and a system that supports fluid, responsive playing.

This chapter is unorthodox because it covers what should be common knowledge. Many would say this chapter should not even exist. But that attitude is the very issue that brought us to this point to begin with. f you're serious about improving your sight-reading, this chapter is essential. It forces you to examine the reality you have versus the reality your sight-reading demands. Until those two align, progress will always feel like an uphill battle.

Sleep: The Silent Partner

Think about the last time you played a piece you knew well, yet still made mistakes. Maybe your fingers felt unresponsive, or your timing was just slightly off. It wasn't a lack of skill—it was exhaustion overriding your precision. Your brain processes and refines muscle memory in deep sleep; without it, your hands won't obey your mind, no matter how much you practice.

Adequate sleep is the foundation of mental sharpness, muscle coordination, and quick decision-making—critical skills for any musician. Research shows that sleep consolidates memory, reinforcing patterns essential for sight-reading and performance. However, sleep disruptions can silently erode these abilities, affecting reaction time, focus, and precision. The following chart breaks down common sleep disruptors and their direct impact on the key components of sight-reading.

Disruptor	Component
Apnea & Snoring	**Neural:** Brain fog reduces reaction time. **Kinetic:** Oxygen deprivation slows muscle response.
Restless Leg Syndrome	**Kinetic:** Impaired leg stability (affects foot pedals). **Neural:** Disrupted sleep cycle reduces focus.
Teeth Grinding	**Auditory:** Jaw tension affects Eustachian tubes. **Neural:** Poor sleep quality diminishes concentration.
Caffeine	**Neural:** Overstimulation delays sleep cycles. **Visual:** Light sleep reduces visual processing speed.
Alcohol	**Neural:** REM disruption stifles learning & memory. **Auditory:** Ear inflammation due to dehydration.
Allergies & Air Quality	**Auditory:** Congestion impacts pitch perception. **Visual:** Oxygen deprivation stifles eye movement.
Late-Night Eating	**Neural:** Raises body temp, delaying deep sleep. **Kinetic:** Poor muscle recovery affects dexterity.
Mid sleep interruption	**Neural:** Poor timing in waking up causes mental fog. **Visual:** Reduces processing speed of notation.

Prompt: Assess your sleep—do you wake up feeling refreshed, or sluggish despite enough rest? Identify disruptors and consider their impact on your focus, coordination, and performance when it comes to sight-reading music. What changes could you implement quickly for fast improvement? Would adjusting your sleep position, refining your bedtime routine, or improving air circulation do the trick? Explore holistic solutions, from mindful breathing to magnesium-rich evening meals, and if issues persist, seek professional guidance with an open mind. Approach it scientifically.

Nutrition: Fueling Peak Performance

Have you ever sat down to practice, only to find your fingers sluggish, your mind foggy, and every note harder than it should be? It's not just your playing—it's your body running on empty. Sleep and nutrition aren't just habits; they're the fuel that determines whether your music soars or stumbles.

Without proper rest and nourishment, even the most disciplined practice falls apart. A well-balanced diet provides sustained energy, sharpens focus, and strengthens coordination—all essential for sight-reading. Compare crashing after coffee and sugar to fueling up with protein, healthy fats, and complex carbs. The difference is night and day. The chart below highlights how key nutrient deficiencies directly impact sight-reading, affecting your ability to process music, react quickly, and maintain endurance.

Deficiency	How It Sabotages Sight-Reading
Iron	**Neural:** Reduced oxygen flow slows mental speed. **Kinetic:** Weakened endurance leads to fatigue.
Magnesium	**Kinetic:** Increased muscle tension and hand cramps. **Neural:** Reduces memory retention & concentration.
B Vitamins	**Neural:** Brain fatigue slows reflexes. **Kinetic:** Poor nerve function reduces coordination.
Omega-3 Fatty Acids	**Neural:** Weak memory retention ad recall. **Auditory:** Diminished auditory processing.
Vitamin D	**Kinetic:** Weak muscle coordination. **Neural:** Mood instability and increased anxiety.
Zinc	**Neural:** Slower problem-solving and adaptability. **Kinetic:** Fatigue, reducing practice stamina.
Glucose Regulation	**Neural:** Energy crashes causing erratic focus. **Visual:** Slow eye tracking hinders notation decoding.
Potassium	**Kinetic:** Muscle fatigue, cramping, and slow reflexes. **Neural:** Poor nerve signaling slows reaction time.

Prompt: Assess your nutrition—have your recent meals supported sustained energy, or have processed foods and quick snacks left you sluggish? Identify how your diet impacts focus, coordination, and endurance during practice. What simple changes could yield fast improvements? Would adding nutrient-dense foods, prepping balanced snacks, or increasing hydration make a difference? Explore holistic solutions, from mindful eating to optimizing meal timing, and if issues persist, seek guidance with an open mind. Approach it scientifically—small adjustments can lead to noticeable performance gains. Experiment, observe, and refine.

Hydration: Activating the Flow

Water is the silent powerhouse behind every cognitive and physical function required for sight-reading. Even mild dehydration can impair focus, reaction time, and muscle coordination, making sight-reading feel sluggish and frustrating. A hydration-first approach enhances sight-reading by keeping all components running efficiently.

Drinking water consistently throughout the day—not just when you feel thirsty—can lead to clearer thinking, better endurance, and sharper execution in your playing. Since music demands sharp mental processing, fine motor control, and auditory precision, hydration directly influences all four key components of sight-reading.Neural: The brain is nearly 75% water, and dehydration slows cognitive function, making note recognition and memory recall sluggish. A well-hydrated brain processes information faster, ensuring fluid sight-reading and quick adaptability to changes in tempo and dynamics.

Kinetic: Muscles and joints rely on proper hydration to function smoothly. Dehydration can cause stiffness, cramps, and reduced finger dexterity, impacting precision in fast passages and making rapid movements feel uncoordinated.

Visual: The eyes depend on hydration to maintain focus and tracking ability. Dehydration can lead to dry eyes and visual fatigue, slowing down reading speed and increasing the likelihood of missing key details in the score.

Auditory: The inner ear relies on fluid balance for proper function. Dehydration can reduce pitch perception and disrupt equilibrium, affecting tuning accuracy and making it harder to adjust to ensemble playing.

Health and Exercise

Once your core systems—rest, fuel, and fluid—are tuned, the next step is to develop a strong, resilient body. Physical health prevents injury, builds endurance, releases tension, and creates the foundation for smooth, efficient movement.

A common Latin expression reads, "Mens sana in corpore sano"—a healthy mind in a healthy body. This timeless phrase underscores the deep connection between physical well-being and mental clarity, both essential for peak sight-reading performance. A well-conditioned body supports sharp focus, smooth coordination, and mental endurance—all essential for sight-reading.

Physical health and fitness are not just about avoiding injury; they directly influence how efficiently you process, react, and execute movements. When the body is strong and balanced, the mind follows, creating a seamless connection between neural processing, kinetic control, visual accuracy, and auditory precision.

Neglecting movement weakens endurance, slows reaction time, and disrupts coordination. Stiffness tightens muscles, fatigue reduces focus, and sluggish neural processing turns quick decisions into hesitation. A strong, mobile body keeps every sight-reading function sharp and responsive. Addressing these issues proactively—through posture awareness, stretching, movement, and proper recovery—ensures that every sight-reading component operates at full capacity.

Prompt: Assess your physical health and activity levels. Are stiffness, fatigue, or discomfort affecting your focus or coordination? Identify two actions—such as improving posture, incorporating daily movement, or optimizing recovery—to enhance endurance and precision. If movement is lacking, choose three enjoyable activities, like stretching, walking, or a physical discipline, to improve resilience. Reflect on any lingering discomfort and how it impacts your performance. What steps can you take this week to address it—adjusting posture, adding recovery techniques, or seeking professional guidance? Your body is your instrument—its health is non-negotiable.

Mindset and Emotions

A strong body supports sharp focus, but without mental clarity, even the most disciplined preparation can fall apart. True mastery comes when the mind and body work together—one without the other creates resistance, hesitation, and inconsistency.

A well-conditioned body creates the foundation for focus, but the mind determines how effortlessly that focus translates into action. Even with optimal sleep, nutrition, hydration, and physical health, mental distractions can unravel precision, disrupt flow, and turn simple tasks into struggles. Emotional discipline and presence are the final layer of control, allowing thoughts to settle so clarity and responsiveness can take over.

An unfocused mind reflects in the body—tension, hesitation, or scattered execution. Frustration, doubt, or external stressors create resistance, leading to erratic decisions and inefficient movement. But just as physical habits shape endurance, mental habits refine presence. The ability to reset, quiet internal noise, and detach from mistakes is what separates struggle from fluidity. A steady, composed mindset allows actions to unfold naturally, without resistance or over-correction.

One of the most effective mental shifts is adopting a Beginner's Mindset—engaging with curiosity rather than fear.

Over-analyzing every step creates hesitation, while trust and adaptability allow for smoother execution. Instead of fixating on perfection, the key is to stay engaged, let mistakes pass without attachment, and move forward without breaking focus. When this mindset is cultivated, presence replaces self-doubt, and clarity replaces overthinking.

Prompt: Consider how your mental state influences your ability to focus and perform under pressure. Do certain thoughts, emotions, or distractions disrupt your clarity? Reflect on recurring patterns—self-doubt, over-analysis, or frustration—and how they impact your flow. Identify one strategy to counteract these barriers, whether through mindfulness, breath control, or a shift in perspective. Could reframing mistakes, practicing detachment, or grounding yourself in the present help? Implement this approach in your next session and observe how it affects your focus, adaptability, and overall performance.

Reflections

Your habits, mindset, and overall well-being define your sight-reading performance. The strategies in this chapter—optimizing sleep, nutrition, movement, hydration, and mental clarity—may seem indirect at first, but they are the foundation of the four sight-reading components: visual, neural, kinetic, and auditory.

When your body is well-rested and properly fueled, your visual processing sharpens, allowing your eyes to scan notation efficiently without strain. A clear and focused mind strengthens the neural component, converting notes into meaningful musical ideas with speed and accuracy. A strong, mobile body ensures the kinetic component functions effortlessly, allowing smooth execution without unnecessary tension. Emotional stability enhances auditory processing, refining your ability to adjust in real-time and respond musically with precision.

This is not a rigid formula—it's a process of refinement. Your role is to observe, experiment, and fine-tune what allows you to perform at your highest level. Small, consistent improvements compound over time, shaping not just your sight-reading, but your overall resilience and adaptability.

Above all, approach this with a sense of ownership and optimism. The challenges you face are not obstacles—they are opportunities to refine your craft and elevate your playing. A balanced, healthy, and focused individual will always perform with greater clarity and confidence. Your music is a direct reflection of your state of being—when you take care of yourself, your playing will follow.

CHAPTER NINE

BECOMING THE MUSICIAN WHO READS EFFORTLESSLY

"THE FUTURE IS NEITHER a prophecy nor a promise—it is a battlefield. It does not wait, it does not care, and it owes you nothing. You can either brace for its impact or step forward and shape it before it arrives. The unprepared fear it. The disciplined create it."

Introduction

The future is not an absolute. It is a canvas shaped by actions. A poor state of mind clings to an outcome, hoping the new reality will conform to expectations. But a prepared mind moves forward—not just adjusting as reality unfolds, but also shaping it. Without controlling or forcing, the prepared mind experiences the future while modifying it through action. This is the difference between waiting for success and ensuring it.

Visualization is not about wishing perfection into existence—it is about training yourself to use imperfection to your advantage. This is no different from sight-reading. If you enter the moment unprepared, you are thrown into uncertainty with no escape. The music is unknown, and hesitation is not an option. Some freeze, because perfection is already out of reach. Others move with certainty—not because they predict every note, but because they trust they are capable, adaptive, and ready. They have already lived the moment before it arrives.

Ultimately, the future is neither fixed nor fake. Do you believe in destiny? If so, then why bother seeking to improve? You might as well surrender to nihilism. But the fact is that the future is yours to generate. It will unfold regardless of your readiness—but when it does, will it meet you on your terms, or will you be at its mercy? What does it mean to prepare for something that does not yet exist? How can you visualize sight-reading a piece of music you have never seen, heard, or even knew about? It always circles back to your mind. Not the notes, not the moment, not the pressure, but the adequate integration to the sight-reading scenario. Your mind is the only thing that can prepare you for what has not yet come.

Shaping Reality

Music is an evolving force, shaped by each performance, each listener, and the countless variables that exist in real-time. No two interpretations are identical, no two audiences hear the same performance in the same way. A musician stands at the center of this dynamic exchange, tasked with delivering an experience that carries both precision and spontaneity. As an interpreter, you are not a passive transmitter of notes but an architect of emotion and energy. The melody may belong to the composer, but the performance belongs to you. You decide whether a phrase soars or sighs, whether the atmosphere feels charged or serene. This control demands simultaneous sensitivity and detachment—the ability to channel emotions into sound without becoming consumed by them. The music must resonate through you, but it cannot overpower you.

Visualization sharpens this skill, training you to direct your energy with intent. Picture yourself sight-reading a new piece for the first time. Before a single note is played, your mind has already scanned the landscape, the phrasing, the harmonic weight, the rhythmic traps. Now, imagine performing that same piece in two vastly different settings: an intimate gathering where subtlety is key, and a grand concert hall where projection and bold gestures take precedence. The same notes, two realities. Your phrasing, dynamics, and even your breathing adjust to fit the space. The essence of visualization lies in shaping these adjustments before they happen, rehearsing not just the physical execution but the mental and emotional command of performance.

By visualizing, you precondition your nervous system to handle unpredictability. You step into the future before it arrives, testing its weight, preparing for its demands. This process is not mere wishful thinking—it is the aikido of performance. You do not resist reality; you guide it. Your weaknesses become strengths, your obstacles, momentum. If you fear highly velocity passages while sight-reading, you might need to train your mind to for unconventional approaches. If you fear the pressure of live performance, rehearse the sensation that shatters the fear. When the time comes, you will enter the moment already victorious.

Every note exists before you touch it. Every sound is first imagined before it is heard. Visualization is not abstract—it is the unseen reality that takes form before the music begins. Controlling that moment means controlling the outcome. But it is not a passive exercise. It must be practiced days, months, and even years in advance so that the sensations and decisions saturate the moment of execution. In sight-reading, visualization must work before, after scanning the score, and during the process itself. It does not manifest through wishful thinking—it materializes only through deliberate, repeated action. Train your mind so reality follows.

Establishing Confidence

Confidence is not an illusion or a gift. It is the atomic fuel that powers resilience, pushing you forward when uncertainty strikes. It is the product of preparation, experience, and self-awareness. It is the certainty that comes from knowing you have put in the work, absorbed the lessons, and built the strength to handle challenging situations. It is not blind faith in ability but trust in what has already been earned through discipline and effort.

Confidence in sight-reading does not stem from isolated success but from repeated exposure to new scores with consistent positive outcomes. It is produced and refined each time you navigate a new piece with clarity and adaptability. Confidence, like fuel, can ignite progress or destruction: misused, it breeds arrogance; unused, it evaporates. But if harnessed with purpose, it forges greatness. When doubt arises, it is often due to a lack of familiarity with a skill or an unresolved weakness in execution. Ignoring these weaknesses allows insecurity to grow; confronting them transforms uncertainty into strength.

The greatest threat to confidence and your music is arrogance—the assumption that ability alone is enough.

Arrogance dismisses growth, avoids critique, and refuses to acknowledge flaws. Humility is the vessel that shields confidence from arrogance. Humility is applied through self-awareness—embracing feedback, acknowledging flaws, and treating growth as an ongoing process. It keeps your mind open to what you have yet to see, sharpening your ability to adapt.

Have you ever heard the expression, "It takes money to make money"? Sight-reading confidence is no different. It must be invested, tested, and refined for it to grow. A plan must be in place, executed with discipline, evaluated with honesty, and strengthened through experience. Be strategic. Tap into its most valuable sources, spend it through continuous execution, and refuel it through reflection rooted in humility. Train with intent, challenge your limits, and refine relentlessly. Build a system where confidence fuels action, action builds experience, and experience regenerates that confidence.

A note on Expectations

The word expectation comes from the Latin ex-pectore, meaning "from the chest," where the heart resides. True expectations are sincere and deeply personal, yet fragile. They require care, not blind hope. A heart that expects recklessly can break. However, when expectation is grounded in clarity and discipline, it becomes a force that shapes the world—it brings reality out of the chest and into motion. When you sight-read, the notes are fixed, but your ability to navigate them must be fluid. If you expect absolute perfection, you invite frustration before you begin. But if you expect to stay present, adapt, and respond musically, you turn the challenge into an opportunity to excel.

Expecting is not the same as wishing. A wish is passive, hoping for an outcome without effort. An expectation, properly cultivated, is a quiet certainty—one that arises from preparation and self-trust. This is the aikido of performance: not forcing reality, but guiding it. When you expect with clarity, confidence, and detachment from rigid outcomes, reality moves toward your vision. The music unfolds, not as an obstacle, but as a path you are already walking.

Visualization and Future-Presence

Everything has led to this final piece of the puzzle in the enigma of sight-reading. From Chapter 1 to Chapter 9, you have refined every variable that shapes your ability to read music in real-time. You have dissected the mechanics, honed your awareness, built resilience, and transformed yourself as a musician. Now, the final step is to turn the key—to bring the future into the present.

A warrior does not wait for battle to study the enemy. Victory is secured long before the first strike. Every strategy, every adjustment, every decision is built in advance so that when the time comes, execution happens without hesitation. This is the most deliberate form of preparation. It takes the raw materials of knowledge, skill, and practice to forge them into something immovable within you. By the time you sit in front of a music stand with a new score, you have already lived the entire battle. Sight-reading in a live setting is the ultimate test of adaptability for any musician, and Future Presence is both your shield and your sword.

Cultivating this ability takes time. It demands discipline, repetition, and clarity of thought. But once you align yourself with this process, the results are undeniable. Now is the moment to implement everything learned, to return to these chapters when needed, to keep yourself in check. Through study, practice, self-awareness, and visualization, you will transform sight-reading from a challenge into second nature. Everything else that scatters your focus should be irrelevant to you now.

But who could be your greatest mentor in this moment? Honestly, the most powerful guide you could ever find is the solid and undeniable sight-reader you are bound to become. The one who knows all your flaws and the buttons that will actually kick you into gear. This mentor has already seen your weaknesses, conquered them, and moved beyond them. The call is now on you to summon the remarkable sight-reader you are to become and to bridge the gap between where you are and where you will be. Mastery is not something that happens to you—it is something you create. The musician who has already conquered this moment is waiting for you. Seek them. Listen to them. Become them.

Reflections

Everything in this book has been about refining your relationship with time. Section 1 planted the seed, but as the chapters progressed, this concept intensified—first by letting go of the past (Chapter 7), then by mastering the present (Chapter 8), and now by stepping into the future before it arrives. This chapter gives you the final edge: the ability to see beyond the immediate, to exist in a moment that hasn't yet happened, and to shape it before it takes form.

Visualization is not a trick. It is the purest form of mental preparation, an act of war against uncertainty. Sight-reading has ceased to be a reaction to something unknown; it becomes the execution of a series of predefined decisions. You are now guided by a version of yourself who has already conquered the challenge. None of this will happen without deliberate practice. Visualization is not a substitute for action. You do not close your eyes, dream of perfection, and wake up transformed. The future is shaped by consistent, disciplined effort, and what you do now determines whether the future plays in your favor or against you. This book has given you the tools—now it is up to you to wield them with precision. Sight-reading is not about playing random pieces and hoping for improvement. It is a system. It is a process. It is war strategy.

Mastering sight-reading is not a matter of chance; it is a process that follows a deliberate strategy. You don't rush in blind. Before playing, you scan the score, identifying key and time signatures, phrasing structures, and rhythmic traps. You separate rhythm and pitch, ensuring they do not compete for your attention. Instead of reading note by note, you recognize entire phrases, harmonic movements, and cadences, processing them as complete thoughts. You start with simplicity, then increase the stakes—timed exercises, ensemble-style practice, and real-time challenges forge sight-reading into a bulletproof state of being. Each of these skills, when reinforced with visualization, removes hesitation entirely. You are no longer reacting to the unknown; you have already seen the notes, anticipated the transitions, and conditioned yourself to execute them with certainty. The moment arrives, and you are prepared.

This is the final chapter of transformation—but your journey doesn't end here. You are no longer the musician who began this process. You have dismantled weaknesses, reshaped habits, and built a mind that no longer hopes for success—it creates it. What comes next is no longer a question of potential—it is a question of execution. The future has already seen you play. And you did not hesitate.

FINALE

The Sight-Reading Breakthrough

Back to the Overture

MASTERING SIGHT-READING IS UNDOUBTEDLY a complex task, and this book has broken it down into three distinct sections to help you navigate its many facets. The goal has always been to increase your awareness of the elements that impact your sight-reading abilities. Reflecting on the journey from the overture to now, you have progressed from unconscious incompetence to conscious incompetence—recognizing areas for improvement and understanding the steps required to move forward.

However, knowledge alone is not enough. Mastery comes not from simply reading but from consistent, intentional application. Sight-reading is a rare and invaluable skill, highly sought after in the musical world, but the only true obstacle in your path is yourself. Take ownership of your growth and commit to the following: Schedule regular evaluations to track your progress. Focus on three specific areas of improvement in each evaluation cycle. Practice patience, allowing yourself time to see results. Engage in weekly public or live sight-reading sessions to build fluency in real-time settings.

This is not a class, and there are no grades to motivate you—your reward will be the tangible improvements in your musicianship. Your journey does not end here. The challenge now is not just to retain what you have learned but to own it, refine it, and apply it in every musical opportunity. The foundation is set. The journey continues.

Training Cycles

Sight-reading fluency develops through deliberate cycles of repetition, assessment, and refinement. It's not about cramming more material—it's about organizing your focus and building strength through precision. This manual encourages a strategic 9-week cycle that ties directly to its structure. Each week, choose one chapter from this book. At the start of the week, take time to evaluate yourself across all the core elements covered in that chapter. Isolate three areas where you are clearly weaker. These will be your focus for the next seven days.

Spend the entire week working specifically on those three elements. Let these weaknesses become your temporary world. What's important to remember is that by going deep into one topic, you'll automatically strengthen others. That's the beauty of interlinked skills. For example, if you focus for a week on understanding Neapolitan chords—what they are, how they resolve, why composers used them—you'll naturally sharpen your vertical scanning ability because now those chords catch your eye. You'll even gain a taste of music history as you notice how differently each composer handled that same harmonic tool. Without ever working directly on stylistic awareness, you've expanded it—just by going all-in on one thing.

After the week ends, move on to a different chapter and repeat the process. Another round of three weaknesses. Another seven days of focused work. Another moment of live testing. By the end of nine weeks, you will have addressed twenty-seven targeted weaknesses—each approached with clarity, depth, and context. Then the cycle repeats. But this time, your assessments will change. What felt like a weakness in the first cycle may now be solid. Other issues will emerge as your perception sharpens. This is where momentum takes over. Every new cycle builds on the last.

What matters most is that you're not trying to fix everything at once. You're deliberately sculpting fluency through structured obsession—one chapter, one week, three elements at a time. Mastery happens slowly, but not randomly. This is how it's built.

Progress Tracking

Keeping track of your development is crucial. Use the following checklist to monitor improvements across technical, mental, and strategic areas:

Technical Mastery – Are you recognizing patterns more quickly? Are rhythms and harmonies becoming more intuitive?
Mental Approach – Are you staying calm under pressure? Do you recover from mistakes without hesitation?

Strategic Growth – Are you applying pre-reading techniques efficiently? Are you scanning for key musical elements before playing?

By tracking these elements consistently, you will see measurable progress and avoid stagnation.

Access Exclusive Sight-Reading Resources

To support your practice and help you stay on track, I've created a set of bonus materials available online. These include printable warm-ups, fluency tracking charts, challenge drills, and more—all structured to enhance your three-week sight-reading cycles. You'll receive immediate access to the Free Expansion Kit, available to all readers. It's a solid starting point for players of all levels and instruments. Start by signing up for the Free Kit first!

Then—if you're feeling ambitious—you can also request access to the format-specific Expansion Kits (eBook, Paperback, Audiobook, NFT, and Hardcover) with extensive additional resources. These include more advanced materials, progressive training modules, and extended drills. Access to these kits is granted manually. Just fill out the request form on the same page to receive a unique 100% discount code based on your book format.

Measuring Your Progress

Self-awareness is the key to growth. This self-evaluation will help you assess your sight-reading abilities across three critical areas: Foundations, Execution, and Personal Growth. By identifying strengths and weaknesses, you can develop a targeted practice strategy. For convenience, an extended version of this evaluation is also in a downloadable PDF version as part of the free resources page. This will allow you to print and track your progress over multiple evaluation cycles.

How to Use This Self-Evaluation

Rate yourself on a scale from 1 to 10 for each question.
Reflect on specific challenges and improvements over time.
If the list feels overwhelming, start with the three most relevant areas for your current level.
Use the three-week training cycle to work on your lowest-scoring areas, then re-evaluate.

Foundation

A strong foundation ensures efficiency and confidence in sight-reading. Assess whether you have mastered the core principles:

Recognizing Patterns: Do you instinctively identify intervals, harmonic structures, and rhythmic groupings?
Scanning Strategies: Have you developed both horizontal (melodic flow) and vertical (harmonic awareness) scanning?
Tempo Confidence: Do you confidently establish a starting tempo based on score analysis?
Technical Awareness: Is your technique refined enough to execute passages fluently at first sight?

Theoretical Understanding: Are you engaging with music theory to reinforce your reading ability?
Contextual Knowledge: Do you research the history and style behind the pieces you sight-read?
Instrument Mastery: Is your instrument an extension of your musical thinking, or does technique still limit you?

If you scored low in this section, focus on strengthening pattern recognition, theoretical knowledge, and scanning techniques before moving forward.

Execution

The ability to sight-read in real-world scenarios requires fluency, adaptability, and interpretative skill. Evaluate how well you execute music under performance conditions:

Rhythmic Interpretation: Do you quickly identify and internalize complex rhythmic patterns?
Harmonic Awareness: Can you pinpoint key harmonic centers and adjust accordingly?
Form & Structure Recognition: Are you able to recognize repetitive motifs, sequences, and phrasing structures at first glance?
Instant Characterization: Can you determine the mood and articulation of a piece instantly?
Expressive Elements: Do you integrate musical expression and dynamics even when reading on the spot?
Voice Differentiation: Can you distinguish and balance melodic, harmonic, and accompaniment lines?
Resilience in Performance: If you make a mistake, do you recover instantly without stopping?

A low score in this section suggests that you should incorporate more live sight-reading experiences and focus on building fluency under pressure.

Growth

Your mindset and habits determine long-term success in sight-reading. Use this section to evaluate your mental approach and overall discipline:

Self-Compassion: Are you forgiving toward mistakes, or do you dwell on them?
Handling Criticism: Do you welcome constructive feedback, or do you become discouraged?
Growth Mindset: Are you actively working on correcting weaknesses, or do you avoid them?
Performance Anxiety: How do you feel when sight-reading in front of others?
Consistency in Practice: Do you sight-read daily, or only when required?
Balance in Musicianship: Does your lifestyle support your growth as a musician?
Visualization & Preparation: Do you mentally prepare and visualize success before performing?

A low score here indicates the need to work on mental resilience, practice consistency, and performance confidence.

What's Next?

Once you've completed your self-evaluation, identify your three weakest areas and make them the focus of your next three-week training cycle. Stay consistent, track your progress, and reassess at the end of each cycle. With structured reflection and focused practice, sight-reading will evolve from a challenge into a reliable, natural skill—one that supports every aspect of your musicianship. Keep evaluating. Keep refining. Keep moving forward.

For your convenience, you can find an Extended Self-Evaluation Worksheet, available inside the Free Expansion Kit.

Sustaining Long-Term Mastery

Sight-reading mastery is not a destination—it is a lifelong process of refinement, adaptability, and continuous learning. As with any skill, progress is not linear, and plateaus are inevitable. The key to sustained improvement lies in reinforcing habits, seeking new challenges, and maintaining an evolving mindset.

Long-Term Strategy for Growth

Reinforce Strong Habits Over Time

Keep a sight-reading routine in your practice schedule, even if only for 10–15 minutes daily.

Rotate between different genres, difficulty levels, and instrumentation to keep skills versatile.

Continue using the three-week training cycles outlined earlier to track and refocus your progress.

Avoiding Plateaus in Progress

Challenge yourself with diverse materials—sight-read pieces beyond your comfort zone.

Increase complexity gradually—experiment with faster tempos, unusual time signatures, and denser harmonies.

Simulate pressure—sight-read in front of others regularly to develop real-time adaptability.

Seek Mentorship and New Challenges

Work with teachers, mentors, or fellow musicians who can provide fresh perspectives and feedback.

Join ensemble groups where sight-reading is essential, such as chamber groups, choirs, or jazz bands.

Set long-term goals, such as mastering a specific style of music or preparing for professional auditions.

The Musician You Were vs. The Musician You Are Becoming

Think back to where you started. Was sight-reading once a source of frustration? Did you hesitate, stumble, or avoid it altogether? Now, you approach the page with confidence, strategy, and control. Your mindset has evolved, and your process has become more structured and intentional.

Take a moment to ask yourself: Would your past self recognize the musician you are today? What breakthroughs have you experienced? What areas still challenge you, and how will you tackle them moving forward? By consistently refining your approach and embracing new challenges, you will ensure that sight-reading remains not just a skill, but a lifelong asset to your musicianship. Keep growing, keep challenging yourself, and let sight-reading open new doors to musical possibilities.

The Final Call to Action

Mastering sight-reading is not an endpoint but a never-ending journey of discovery. Each new piece you encounter is an opportunity—an invitation to explore, interpret, and connect with music in real time. The true reward of sight-reading is not perfection, but freedom. By now, you have transformed your approach. Sight-reading is no longer a test—it is a gateway to greater musicianship. It allows you to adapt quickly, perform with confidence, and engage with music beyond the notes on the page. The more you trust the process, the more natural and intuitive it becomes.

The path forward is simple: keep going. Keep refining your skills, embracing challenges, and pushing past limitations. If a passage feels difficult, remember that every great musician has stood where you are now at some point. The only difference between those who master sight-reading and those who don't is consistent, deliberate practice. Approach each new piece with curiosity and confidence. Let every challenge refine your instincts, every mistake teach resilience, and every success fuel your passion. The skills you have built here will serve you for a lifetime—but only if you use them.

The next page is waiting. Turn it, and keep playing.

YOUR JOURNEY FORWARD

It Doesn't End Here

Congratulations on dedicating yourself to the art of sight-reading. Taking this skill seriously is a major step toward becoming a more versatile and confident musician. Competence and excellence, as you've discovered, are easier to talk about than to achieve. But the journey you've started here lays a strong foundation—if you commit to the work it demands.

The principles and techniques outlined in these pages demand consistent application and refinement. Sight-reading, requires practice, patience, and intention. Without forming habits that reinforce what you've learned, progress will stall. The true power of this book lies not in its words but in the actions you take to integrate its lessons into your daily musical practice. As your sight-reading improves, you may find yourself tempted to rely more on memorization. Embrace this as part of the learning process. Memorization stretches your brain and helps you uncover patterns, connections, and parallels between pieces. Use those newly "memorized" pieces to expand your spontaneity and adaptability by reading them again with a different approach.

This book is meant to be a resource you return to throughout your musical journey. Reengage with the sections that challenge you, explore the exercises again, and reflect on how your understanding evolves. Every time you revisit this material, you'll find new insights that align with where you are in your growth. Progress is not about perfection but about persistence. As Aesop reminds us in the fable *The Tortoise and the Hare:* "Slow but steady wins the race." Commit yourself to consistent, effective effort, and you will see the results. The rewards of sight-reading fluency—the confidence, opportunities, and freedom it brings—are well worth the investment.

Now, take what you've learned, apply it, and build habits that will support your growth. Music is a lifelong journey, and sight-reading is a skill that will serve you every step of the way. Keep practicing, keep exploring, and keep playing with passion. The next chapter of your musical story is yours to write.

THE TEAM

AUTHOR, EDITOR, AND CONTRIBUTORS

Luciano Marazzo - Author

LUCIANO MARAZZO IS A classically trained musician, educator, and advocate for the arts from Buenos Aires, Argentina. His career combines performance, mentorship, and community-building, making him a multifaceted figure in the musical world. He has performed globally as an opera singer and classical guitarist, captivating audiences with his artistry and passion. As a teacher, Luciano is dedicated to fostering talent and opening doors for musicians to realize their potential, emphasizing the transformative power of music in personal and professional growth.

Luciano is the founder of Ascoltando, Inc., a 501(c)(3) nonprofit organization that promotes the arts and supports individuals who are hard of hearing. Among its many initiatives, the Online Music Guild—a project of Ascoltando—offers a platform for musicians to connect, learn, and grow, transcending geographical boundaries. Through this project, Luciano has created opportunities for artists worldwide, cultivating a vibrant and supportive musical community.

His dedication to education stems from a lifelong commitment to music. He began his studies in piano at the age of seven under Silvia Leidemann and later transitioned to classical guitar, studying with the esteemed Irma Costanzo. These early experiences laid the foundation for his technical expertise and interpretative depth. After moving to the United States, Luciano refined his craft under the guidance of Tobin Roye, Renato Serrano, and Tom Patterson, further honing his skills as a classical guitarist.

As an opera singer, Luciano's artistry has been shaped by world-class mentors. His first vocal coach, the renowned Chinese opera star Dr. Ying Yeh, guided him through critical stages of his development, helping him earn awards, a degree, and a Vocal Pedagogy Certificate. Additional mentorship from Pamela Bathurst, Pamela Casella, Marilyn Curtis, and Grayson Hirst further enriched his vocal technique and performance acumen.

Luciano's mission extends beyond personal achievement. He is passionate about creating opportunities for musicians to thrive, whether through his nonprofit work, educational initiatives, or performances. His belief in the power of music to inspire and unite drives his work, making him a benefactor of the arts and a champion for the next generation of musicians.

Gustavo Beaklini – Foreword

Gustavo Beaklini is an award-winning harpist from Brazil whose career has taken him to stages across the globe. As a performer, he has captivated audiences with his solo, chamber, and symphonic work, earning recognition for his technical brilliance and artistic sensitivity.

In 2008, Gustavo achieved a significant milestone when he was appointed Principal Harpist of the Symphonic Orchestra of Theatro da Paz in Belém. This prestigious role marked a pivotal moment in his career, laying the foundation for his continued success as a performer and musician.

Among Gustavo's numerous accolades are the XVI Young Soloists Competition of the Symphonic Orchestra of Porto Alegre and the Soloists Competition of the Symphonic Orchestra of the Federal University of Rio de Janeiro. These achievements underscore his dedication to his craft and his standing as one of Brazil's most distinguished harpists.

Michael DeMers – Contributor

Michael DeMers is a composer of contemporary orchestral and chamber music, as well as a seasoned trombonist and dedicated music educator. His compositional style is best described as a twentieth-century reinterpretation of traditional Romantic and Classical forms and structures, seamlessly blending historical influences with modern sensibilities.

A hallmark of Michael's artistry is his focus on imagery and visualization. He draws inspiration from observing the natural beauty and intricate narratives of life, believing that these elements are key to fueling creativity across all artistic disciplines. His works often reflect a deep connection to the world around him, translating complex emotions and vivid imagery into compelling musical experiences.

Michael's dedication to education is evident in his belief that the pursuit of knowledge is a lifelong endeavor for any artist. While the timeline for formal degrees may be finite, his drive to learn and inspire through teaching remains boundless. This commitment to both artistry and education cements his role as a vital figure in contemporary music.

Kevin Valenzuela – Contributor

Kevin Valenzuela is a multifaceted music professional, combining his expertise as a music teacher, composer, and recording studio manager. With a deep understanding of the music industry, Kevin recognizes the critical importance of strong sight-reading skills in fostering adaptability and excellence in musicianship.

Kevin's extensive vocal and instrumental experience has established him as an accomplished sight-singer, a skill that has profoundly influenced his teaching and creative endeavors. His contributions to Music at First Sight were instrumental in shaping the book's second section, offering practical strategies and insights that draw from his real-world expertise and commitment to empowering musicians.

Eric James Seiler – Contributor

Eric James Seiler is a distinguished vocalist, choir director, and educator with an impressive academic and professional background. He holds a Master of Music and Certificate in Vocal Pedagogy from California State University, Chico, as well as a Master of Education from National University. With a career that spans performances in 27 countries, Eric's work reflects both versatility and dedication to his craft.

As the director of a chamber choir that has performed by invitation at Carnegie Hall, Eric has consistently demonstrated excellence in leadership and musical interpretation. His global experiences and expertise in vocal pedagogy provide invaluable perspectives on the challenges and rewards of mastering sight-reading.

Eric's contributions to Music at First Sight enriched the book with practical insights and a deep understanding of the role sight-reading plays in both individual and ensemble settings. His passion for empowering musicians shines through in his commitment to helping others overcome the complexities of this essential skill.

Nune Melik – Contributor

Nuné Melik is a multifaceted artist whose career exemplifies the limitless possibilities of artistic expression. As a soloist, she has graced prestigious stages, including Carnegie Hall and the United Nations Headquarters, captivating audiences with her dynamic performances. Touring internationally since the age of nine, Nuné has continually expanded her musical and creative horizons.

Beyond her work as a performer, Nuné is deeply committed to humanitarian efforts, music education, and artistic exploration through poetry, acting, and directing. Her passion for nurturing talent extends to her role as an expert coach, where she guides performers in overcoming stage fright and developing reliable, confident performance practices.

Nuné's contributions to Music at First Sight bring invaluable insights into the mental and emotional aspects of performance, inspiring readers to embrace artistry with courage and authenticity.

Jessica Muiseke-Wilkison – Contributor

Jessica Muiseke-Wilkison is a dedicated educator, performer, and advocate for underperformed works in the standard repertoire. A certified member of the Arizona String Teachers Association, Jessica has over a decade of teaching experience, specializing in violin, theory, and composition. As the former lead teacher of the Arizona String Project, she has played a significant role in mentoring young musicians and fostering a love for string performance.

Jessica's passion for early music is evident through her performances with Arizona Baroque and the Arizona Symphony Orchestra, where she seeks out and champions lesser-known works. Beyond the concert stage, she has been a featured recording artist on independent film scores, video game soundtracks, and numerous indie, pop, and metal albums, showcasing her versatility and commitment to expanding the boundaries of classical music.

Jessica's contributions to Music at First Sight bring a fresh perspective on integrating sight-reading with creative expression and ensemble work. Her dedication to education and her innovative approach to performance make her an invaluable part of the book's vision for empowering musicians.

Printed in Dunstable, United Kingdom

77242092R00088